26 Champ
ROSARy

To Jane,
Pat,

Fr Donald ~~~~

THE ESSENTIAL GUIDE TO THE GREATEST HEROES OF THE ROSARY

Donald H. Calloway, MIC

Available from:
Marian Helpers Center
Stockbridge, MA 01263

Prayerline: 1-800-804-3823
Orderline: 1-800-462-7426
Websites: fathercalloway.com
marian.org

Publication Date:
August 2, 2017

Imprimi Potest:
Very Rev. Kazimierz Chwalek, MIC
Provincial Superior
The Blessed Virgin Mary, Mother of Mercy Province
May 31, 2017

Nihil Obstat:
Dr. Robert A. Stackpole, STD
Censor Deputatus
May 31, 2017

Library of Congress Catalog Number: 2017907833
ISBN: 978-1-59614-401-9

Cover image is taken from *The 26 Champions of the Rosary* by Maria
Madonna Bouza Urbina. (2016). Commissioned by Fr. Donald H.
Calloway, MIC. www.fathercalloway.com

Cover design and inside pages layout by Kathy Szpak

Editing and Proofreading:
Michelle Buckman; Chris Sparks; Robert Stackpole, STD;
Joan Lamar; Andy Leeco; Melanie Williams

Acknowledgments: Marian Fathers of the Immaculate Conception;
Mr. and Mrs. Donald & LaChita Calloway; Matthew T. Calloway;
Ileana E. Salazar; Teresa de Jesus Macias; Milanka Lachman;
Theresa Vonderschmitt

Printed in the United States of America

Dedicated to

Teresa de Jesús Macías
(Mamita)
Thank you for opening your heart and home to me.
May your reward be great in heaven!

26 Champions of the Rosary
The Essential Guide to the Greatest Heroes of the Rosary

Introduction 7

Champions of the Rosary 11

St. Dominic (1170–1221) 13
Blessed Alan de la Roche (1428–1475) 22
St. Pope Pius V (1504–1572) 29
St. Louis de Montfort (1673–1716) 34
St. Alphonsus Liguori (1696–1787) 41
Blessed Pope Pius IX (1792–1878) 46
St. Anthony Mary Claret (1807–1870) 51
Pope Leo XIII (1810–1903) 58
Blessed Bartolo Longo (1841–1926) 66
Servant of God Joseph Kentenich (1885–1968) 73
Servant of God Lúcia Dos Santos (1907–2005) 79
St. Maximilian Kolbe (1894–1941) 86
Servant of God Frank Duff (1889–1980) 94
Pope Pius XI (1857–1939) 99
Blessed James Alberione (1884–1971) 105
Venerable Pope Pius XII (1876–1958) 114
Servant of God Dolindo Ruotolo (1882–1970) 122
St. Pio of Pietrelcina (1887–1968) 127
St. Josemaria Escrivá (1902–1975) 132
St. Pope John XXIII (1881–1963) 137
Servant of God Patrick Peyton (1909–1992) 142
Blessed Pope Paul VI (1897–1978) 149
Venerable Fulton J. Sheen (1895–1979) 155
St. Teresa of Calcutta (1910–1997) 161
St. John Paul II (1920–2005) 166
Pope Benedict XVI (1927–present) 175

HOW TO CHAMPION THE ROSARY 183

How to Become a Champion of the Rosary 185

Why Pray the Rosary? 190

How to Pray the Rosary 196

Praying the Rosary 200

Prayers of the Rosary 201

Mysteries of the Rosary 203

Joyful Mysteries 203

Luminous Mysteries 204

Sorrowful Mysteries 206

Glorious Mysteries 208

The 15 Promises of Our Lady to Those Who Pray

the Rosary 210

Indulgences of the Rosary 212

References 215

INTRODUCTION

I love the rosary so much! I'll never be able to say enough about the power and wonder of the blessed beads of Our Lady. This explains why I spent three years researching and writing what I consider to be my best book, *Champions of the Rosary: The History and Heroes of a Spiritual Weapon* (to order this book, see page 246). In *Champions of the Rosary*, I present a complete history of the rosary, helpful hints on how to pray the rosary, and 26 of the rosary's greatest champions. In many ways, it was the 26 champions that captivated readers and had many people asking me to publish this section in a separate, smaller book.

Who are these champions? They are the ones who stand out in the 800-year history of the rosary as the main promoters and heroes of the Church's preeminent form of devotion to Our Lady: the rosary. The first champion was St. Dominic. In addition to founding the rosary, he also founded the Order of Preachers (Dominicans). He was a holy priest, and Our Lady first entrusted the powerful spiritual sword of the rosary to him. After him, there have been numerous others who have championed this devotion and help spread it to the ends of the earth. There are even papal champions, like St. Pope Pius V. This incredible pope is responsible for saving Western Civilization from Islamic takeover, and he did it through the rosary and a Holy League of men willing to defend Christianity. Other papal champions of the rosary, such as Pope Leo XIII and St. John Paul II, wrote important documents on the rosary and helped spread the devotion far and wide — Pope Leo XIII wrote 11 encyclicals on the rosary, and St. John Paul II re-sharpened the ancient blade of the rosary by turning it into a modern day lightsaber with his institution of the Luminous Mysteries.

History has also witnessed saints like St. Louis de Montfort and St. Anthony Mary Claret champion the rosary. Saint Louis de Montfort wrote one of the greatest books ever written on the rosary, and Saint Anthony Mary mandated that every priest in his diocese pray the rosary with their parishioners on Sundays and solemnities. For his zeal in promoting the rosary, Our Lady appeared to St. Anthony Mary Claret on several occasions and declared him to be a "new St. Dominic." Similar to St. Louis de Montfort, St. Josemaria Escriva wrote a magnificent book on the rosary, while St. Pio of Pietrelcina and St. Teresa of Calcutta gave witness to the blessed beads by almost always having a rosary in their hands.

One of the most amazing stories of the power of the rosary is from a man who was once an ordained Satanic priest! He was from Naples, Italy, and his name is Blessed Bartolo Longo. After his radical return to Catholicism — which he attributed to the rosary — he began construction on what would become the famous shrine of Our Lady of the Rosary of Pompeii. His love for Jesus and Mary knew no bounds, and he also initiated many works of mercy to help orphans, widows, and the sick. Then there's the Servant of God Frank Duff, founder of the world's largest Marian apostolate, the Legion of Mary. He required all members of the Legion to pray the rosary; Mao Tse-tung, the Communist leader and father of the People's Republic of China, once referred to the Legion of Mary as "Public Enemy Number One."

While there are many champions of the rosary throughout history who were unable to read or write — this explains why there are only 26 champions presented in this book, and only 2 women — nonetheless, one of the visionaries of Fatima, the Servant of God Sr. Lucia Dos Santos, was explicitly instructed by Our Lady to learn how to read and write in order to promote the rosary to the world. And perhaps one of the most inspiring champions in the long-litany of rosary promoters was the Servant of God Patrick Peyton. This holy priest gathered more people together to pray the rosary than any other person in Church history. Through his heroic efforts, millions of people gathered in the streets of Brazil, Colombia, and the Philippines to pray the rosary and peacefully overcome political dictators and ideological regimes; he even gathered half a million people in a park in San Francisco to pray the rosary in 1961.

This is just a sampling of the great champions of the rosary that you will find in this book. But, in some way, this book is not only about them, but also about you. What you will discover in these pages is that you, too, are capable of being listed among their company! By praying the rosary and promoting it, you can be a champion and a hero of the rosary of Our Lady!

Who, dear reader, will wield the spiritual sword of the rosary for the Queen of Heaven today and become a champion against the darkness of our present times? Is it you?

Very Rev. Donald Calloway, MIC, STL
Vicar Provincial — Marian Fathers of the Immaculate Conception
The Blessed Virgin Mary, Mother of Mercy Province

THE 26 CHAMPIONS OF THE ROSARY

CHAMPIONS OF
THE ROSARY

I want no respite in this battle, but I shall fight to the last breath for the glory of my King and Lord. I shall not lay the sword aside until he calls me before his throne; I fear no blows, because God is my shield.

~ St. Faustina Kowalska

Put on the whole armor of God, that you may be able to stand against the wiles of the devil. For we are not contending against flesh and blood, but against the principalities, against the powers, against the world rulers of this present darkness, against the spiritual hosts of wickedness in the heavenly places. Therefore take up the whole armor of God, so that you may be able to withstand on the evil day, and having done everything, to stand firm. Stand therefore, and fasten the belt of truth around your waist, and put on the breastplate of righteousness. As shoes for your feet put on whatever will make you ready to proclaim the gospel of peace. With all of these, take the shield of faith, with which you will be able to quench all the flaming arrows of the evil one. And take the helmet of salvation, and the sword of the Spirit, which is the word of God.

~ Ephesians 6:11-17

ST. DOMINIC

The Founder of the Rosary
1170–1221

CANONIZED: July 3, 1234 by Pope Gregory IX
FEAST DAY: August 8

SAINT DOMINIC, born in Caleruega, Spain, was the founder of the Order of Preachers. His mother, Blessed Juana of Aza, while still carrying him in her womb, had a vision of a dog setting the world on fire with a torch that it carried in its mouth. The vision proved to be prophetic. In 1216, St. Dominic founded the Dominicans, who quickly became known as the *Domini canes* (the dogs of God). A renowned preacher of Christian truths, St. Dominic founded the "dogs of God" to be a band of well-formed itinerant preachers, sniffing out heresy and bringing the lost sheep of God's flock back to pasture. Through his preaching, St. Dominic was able to bring back many souls from the errors of the Albigensian heresy. He died at age 51 in Bologna, Italy.

Marian Devotion

Saint Dominic was a Marian saint who, as he walked from town to town preaching the Gospel, raised his voice in song to Our Lady by preaching her Psalter and singing the *Ave Maris Stella* (Hail, Star of the Sea). His early biographers mention that he frequently received visions of the Virgin Mary and preached about her with great fervor. In one particular vision, Jesus himself informed St. Dominic that the Dominicans were entrusted to the protection of Mary. According to Dominican tradition, part of the Dominican habit itself is said to have been given to the order by Our Lady. Saint Dominic's tender devotion to the Virgin Mary is considered to be the very foundation upon which the Order of Preachers rests. His love for Mary is further evidenced by the fact that the primitive Constitutions of the Order required all the members to profess obedience to both God *and* the Virgin Mary.

Pope Benedict XVI, in a general audience on February 3, 2010, summarized the primary elements that went into making the life and apostolic action of St. Dominic fruitful and made clear that St. Dominic's devotion to Mary took pride of place. The pope said: "In the very first place is Marian devotion which he [St. Dominic] fostered tenderly and left as a precious legacy to his spiritual sons who, in the history of the Church, have had the great merit of disseminating the prayer of the holy rosary, so dear to the Christian people and so rich in Gospel values: a true school of faith and piety."

Champion of the Rosary

According to the Dominican tradition, St. Dominic founded the rosary in the year 1208. After having devoted all his efforts to trying to win back the hearts and minds of those who had been swept away by the Albigensian heresy, St. Dominic retreated to a forest near Prouille, France, to seek guidance from heaven. It was there that the Virgin Mary entrusted the rosary to St. Dominic, instructing him in its use and implementation, and effectively making him the father of a new form of preaching and praying. With the spiritual sword of the rosary in his hand, St. Dominic's new style of preaching became effective against the Albigensians and won many back to the fullness of Christian teaching in the Catholic Church.

As part of her instructions to St. Dominic about the rosary, the Queen of Heaven informed him that the rosary was to be understood as a weapon of war and a battering ram against heresy. With this in mind, St. Dominic founded the Order of Preachers, a band of brothers known as the "dogs of God" and the Order of the Rosary. In time, the rosary would be officially recognized as part of the Dominican habit and worn on the left side in order to symbolize a sword ready to be unsheathed and taken into spiritual combat. The greatest stories of the power and effectiveness of the rosary in the life of St. Dominic are recorded in *The Secret of the Rosary* by the Third Order Dominican St. Louis de Montfort.

Saint Dominic is also credited with founding the Confraternity of the Rosary. In his zeal for promoting truth and saving souls, St. Dominic founded this association of prayer to accompany the rosary and assure its spread throughout the world. Much like the rosary itself, this movement was initially known by various other names and titles. Yet it has been affirmed by many popes that this confraternity of prayer was originally founded by St. Dominic. In all likelihood, the Confraternity of the Rosary began in the Church of St. Sixtus in Rome in 1216 and was brought to other countries such as Spain and France by St. Dominic himself.

Rosary Gems

Wonder not that until now you [St. Dominic] have obtained so little fruit by your labors; you have spent them on a barren soil, not yet watered with the dew of divine grace. When God willed to renew the face of the earth, he began by sending down on it the fertilizing rain of the Angelic Salutation. Therefore, preach my Psalter.

~ Our Lady's words to St. Dominic

Through the merits of the Virgin Mary herself and the intercession of Saint Dominic, [who was] once the excellent preacher of this Confraternity of the Rosary, this entire world was preserved.

~ Pope Alexander VI

The Albigensian heresy, then raging in a part of France, had blinded so many of the laity that they were cruelly attacking priests and clerics. Blessed Dominic lifted his eyes to heaven and turned them toward the Virgin Mary, the Mother of God. Dominic invented this method of prayer, which is easy and suitable to everyone and which is called the Rosary or the Psalter of the Blessed Virgin Mary. It consists of venerating the Blessed Virgin by reciting 150 Angelic Salutations, the same number as the Psalms of David, interrupting them at each decade by the Lord's Prayer, meanwhile meditating on the mysteries which recall the entire life of our Lord Jesus Christ. After having devised it, Dominic and his sons spread this form of prayer throughout the Church.

~ St. Pope Pius V

When he [St. Dominic] had been advised by her [Our Lady], as the tradition says, that he should preach the rosary to the people as a singular protection against heresies and vices, he carried out the task enjoined on him with wonderful fervor and success.

~ Servant of God Pope Benedict XIII

Saint Dominic, seeing that the gravity of people's sins was hindering the conversion of the Albigensians, withdrew into a forest near Toulouse where he prayed unceasingly for three days and three nights. During this time he did nothing but weep and do harsh penances in order to appease the anger of Almighty God. He used his discipline so much that his body was lacerated, and finally he fell into a coma. At this point Our Lady appeared to him, accompanied by three angels, and she said: "Dear Dominic, do you know which weapon the Blessed Trinity wants to use to reform the world?" "Oh, my Lady," answered Saint Dominic, "you know far better than I do because next to your Son Jesus Christ you have always been the chief instrument of our salvation." Then Our Lady replied: "I want you to know that, in this kind of warfare, the battering ram has always been the Angelic Psalter [the Hail Mary] which is the foundation stone of the New Testament. Therefore if you want to reach these hardened souls and win them over to God, preach my Psalter."

~ St. Louis de Montfort

As long as priests followed Saint Dominic's example and preached devotion to the holy rosary, piety and fervor thrived throughout the Christian world and in those religious orders which were devoted to the rosary. But since people have neglected this gift from heaven, all kinds of sin and disorder have spread far and wide.

~ St. Louis de Montfort

All during life, Saint Dominic had nothing more at heart than to praise Our Lady, to preach her greatness and to inspire everybody to honor her by saying the rosary.

~ St. Louis de Montfort

Saint Dominic was so convinced of the efficacy of the holy rosary and of its great value that, when he heard confessions, he hardly ever gave any other penance.

~ St. Louis de Montfort

Blanche of Castille, Queen of France, was deeply grieved because twelve years after her marriage she was still childless. When Saint Dominic went to see her he advised her to say her rosary every day to ask God for the grace of motherhood, and she faithfully carried out his advice. In 1213 she gave birth to her eldest child, Philip, but the child died in infancy. The Queen's fervor was nowise dulled by this disappointment; on the contrary, she sought Our Lady's help more than ever before. She had a large number of rosaries given out to all members of the court and also to people in several cities of the kingdom, asking them to join her in entreating God for a blessing that this time would be complete. Thus, in 1215, Saint Louis was born — the prince who was to become the glory of France and the model of all Christian kings.

~ St. Louis de Montfort

When our Blessed Lady gave the holy rosary to Saint Dominic she ordered him to say it every day and to get others to say it daily. Saint Dominic never let anyone join the Confraternity unless he were fully determined to say it every day.

~ St. Louis de Montfort

After St. Dominic had founded the Order of Preachers, it was his desire to put an end to the errors of the Albigensians. Moved by divine inspiration, he began to implore the help of the Immaculate Mother of God, to whom alone it has been given to wipe out all the heresies in the universe, and he preached the rosary as an infallible protection against heresies and vices.

~ Blessed Pope Pius IX

You know how the [rosary] devotion came about; how, at a time when heresy was very widespread, and had called in the aid of sophistry, that can so powerfully aid infidelity against religion, God inspired St. Dominic to institute and spread this devotion. It seems so simple and easy, but you know God chooses the small things of the world to humble the great. Of course, it was first of all for the poor and simple, but not for them only, for everyone who has practiced the devotion knows that there is in it a soothing sweetness that there is in nothing else.

~ Blessed John Henry Newman

Under her [Mary's] inspiration, strong with her might, great men were raised up — illustrious for their sanctity no less than for their apostolic spirit — to beat off the attacks of wicked adversaries and to lead souls back into the virtuous ways of Christian life, firing them with a consuming love of the things of God. One such man, an army in himself, was Dominic Guzman [St. Dominic]. Putting all his trust in Our Lady's rosary, he set himself fearlessly to the accomplishment of both these tasks with happy results.

~ Pope Leo XIII

Great in the integrity of his doctrine, in his example of virtue, and by his apostolic labors, he [St. Dominic] proceeded undauntedly to attack the enemies of the Catholic Church, not by force of arms; but trusting wholly to that devotion which he was the first to institute under the name of the holy rosary, which was disseminated through the length and breadth of the earth by him and his pupils. Guided, in fact, by divine inspiration and grace, he foresaw that this devotion, like a most powerful warlike weapon, would be the means of putting the enemy to flight, and of confounding their audacity and mad impiety. Such was indeed its result. Thanks to this new method of prayer — when adopted and properly carried out as instituted by the Holy Father St. Dominic — piety, faith, and union began to return, and the projects and devices of the heretics to fall to pieces. Many wanderers also returned to the way of salvation, and the wrath of the impious was restrained by the arms of those Catholics who had determined to repel their violence.

~ Pope Leo XIII

That great saint [St. Dominic], divinely enlightened, perceived that no remedy would be more adapted to the evils of his time than that men should return to Christ, who "is the way, the truth, and the life," by frequent meditation on the salvation obtained for us by him, and should seek the intercession with God of that Virgin, to whom it is given to destroy all heresies. He therefore so composed the rosary as to recall the mysteries of our salvation in succession, and the subject of meditation is mingled and, as it were, interlaced with the Angelic Salutation and with the prayer addressed to God, the Father of Our Lord Jesus Christ.

~ Pope Leo XIII

The Mother of God taught the rosary to the patriarch [St.] Dominic in order that he might propagate it.

~ Pope Leo XIII

Loving the Blessed Virgin as a Mother, confiding chiefly in her patronage, Dominic started his battle for the Faith. The Albigenses, among other dogmas, attacked both the Divine maternity and the virginity of Mary. He, attacked by them with every insult, defending to the utmost of his strength the sanctity of these dogmas, invoked the help of the Virgin Mother herself, frequently using these words: "Make me worthy to praise thee, Sacred Virgin; give me strength against thine enemies." How pleased was the Heavenly Queen with her pious servant may be easily gathered from this, that she used his ministry to teach the most holy rosary to the Church, the Spouse of her Son; that prayer which, being both vocal and mental, in the contemplation especially of the mysteries of religion. Rightly, then, did Dominic order his followers, in preaching to the people, to inculcate frequently this manner of prayer, the utility of which he had experienced.

~ Pope Benedict XV

The battle around the humanity of Christ begins anew with the Albigensians in the Middle Ages. St. Dominic steps forth and selects as foundation for his effectiveness the proclamation of the faith in the illustrious motherhood of Mary, the frequent repetition of the Hail Mary. The rosary becomes a Summa Theologica, *a catechism for the people which has the double character of being both a prayer and teacher. From it, the Dominican preachers drew both the contents and armor for their sermons.*

~ Servant of God Joseph Kentenich

To her [Mary] is given the office of destroying heresies throughout the world. Dominic received from her, according to tradition, the admonition to preach the rosary as a singularly effective weapon against heresy and vice, and the fervor and success with which he carried out the task entrusted to him are truly amazing.

~ Blessed James Alberione

In his spirituality, St. Dominic used to have recourse also to material means in prayer; and among other endeavors he made use of the beads to count the "Hail Marys." Then, noting the people's ignorance concerning religion, and having to combat the Albigensians who denied the fundamental truths of Christianity, Dominic, inspired by God, thought it well to have the people meditate a truth or mystery every ten "Hail Marys." Thus, while giving to the people an easy manner of praying, he also gave a simple means of instruction.

~ Blessed James Alberione

St. Dominic wanted these mysteries [of the rosary] recalled every day, that they might be well impressed on the mind and never be forgotten.

~ Blessed James Alberione

St. Dominic, who died in 1221, received from the Blessed Mother the command to preach and to popularize this devotion [the rosary] for the good of souls, for conquest over evil, and for the prosperity of Holy Mother Church and thus gave us the rosary in its present classical form.

~ Venerable Fulton J. Sheen

The tradition given great weight by many popes has it that early in the thirteenth century the Blessed Mother told St. Dominic to preach the rosary. By means of this formidable weapon he was able to roll back another great tide of heresy threatening the Church, and with St. Francis of Assisi, to leave a revitalized faith to the Middle Ages.

~ Servant of God Patrick J. Peyton

The traditional image of Our Lady of the Rosary portrays Mary with one arm supporting the Child Jesus and with the other offering the rosary beads to Saint Dominic. This important iconography shows that the rosary is a means given by the Virgin to contemplate Jesus and, in meditating on his life, to love him and follow him ever more faithfully.

~ Pope Benedict XVI

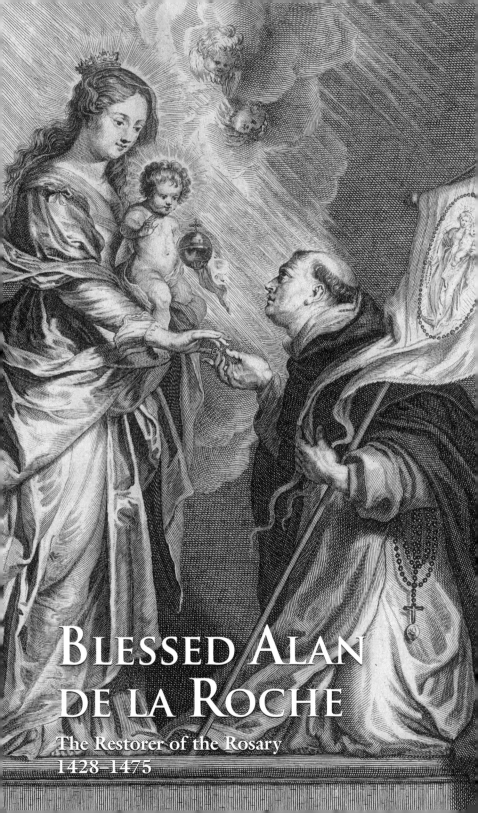

BLESSED ALAN DE LA ROCHE

The Restorer of the Rosary
1428–1475

B LESSED ALAN DE LA ROCHE was born in Brittany and entered the Dominicans at an early age. He was a faithful spiritual son of St. Dominic. After making his profession of vows, he studied in Paris, where he became a distinguished lecturer of sacred theology. As a priest, he taught theology in Lille, Douai, and Ghent, and at one point was also designated by his superiors to serve as the official visitor for Dominican houses in central Europe. He was a renowned preacher and got involved in the Observant Reform Movement within the Dominicans that sought to return their order to the faithful observance of the ideals of their founder. Blessed Alan died on September 8, 1475, the Feast of Our Lady's Birth, in Zwolle, Holland.

The Dominicans have traditionally accorded Alan the title of "Blessed," and he is universally acclaimed by the Church as such, though he has never been formally beatified. In certain countries, Catholic parishes have been named after him and have even bestowed on him the title "St. Alan." There are many devotional statues depicting Bl. Alan in churches around the world, and many Dominican priests and brothers continue to take "Alan" as part of their religious name. In the old Dominican Breviary, Bl. Alan was celebrated with a special feast day. Today, though he has no official feast, he is unofficially honored on the date of his death, September 8.

Marian Devotion

According to Dominican tradition, Bl. Alan experienced a deeper conversion of life through the intercession of the Blessed Virgin Mary. In *The Secret of the Rosary,* the Third Order Dominican St. Louis de Montfort noted that, in his youth, Bl. Alan was horribly tempted by devils and fell into many sins, but, through Mary's intercession, was given the ability to overcome Satan and his devices. The English translation of Bl. Alan's name is "Alan of the Rock." After his conversion, he adhered firmly to the teachings of the Church, joined the Dominicans, and became a devout friar and zealous preacher in the service of the Queen of Heaven. It is said that during his priestly life, he never began any endeavor, whether mundane or sacred, without first saying a Hail Mary.

Blessed Alan's love for Mary was so intense that, like many other chivalric saints, he was given the title "new spouse of Mary." His love for the Virgin of virgins was so pure and virtuous that he was considered another St. Joseph. Other Marian saints who were privileged to bear this same title include St. Edmund Rich, St. Hermann Joseph, and St. John Eudes. For his part, in his visions, Bl. Alan was even given a necklace made of Mary's hair and presented with a ring that symbolized the spiritual marriage existing between himself and the Virgin. In one of his visions, Mary appeared to him and placed the ring on his finger herself. (See the image on the previous page for an artistic depiction of this event.)

Champion of the Rosary

During his life, Bl. Alan received many visions from Jesus, Mary, and St. Dominic. Almost all of these visions centered on the rosary and heaven's desire for him to renew it. Commanded and commissioned to be the one to restore the rosary devotion, Bl. Alan was at first reluctant to follow heaven's directions. It was only after being rebuked by Jesus for having the knowledge and influence as a son of St. Dominic to bring about a renewal in the rosary and failing to do so that Bl. Alan put all his fears behind him and became the great restorer of the rosary devotion and the Confraternity of the Rosary.

In order to restore the rosary and its Confraternity, Bl. Alan wrote several historical books and manuals that taught others how to pray the rosary. His manuals helped to bring about the restoration of the Confraternity of the Rosary in Douai, France, in 1470. Five years after his successful renewal of the rosary and its Confraternity, his Dominican confrere Fr. Jacob Sprenger established a confraternity in Cologne, Germany, on September 8, 1475, the very day that Bl. Alan died. The confraternity in Cologne would be the first officially recognized confraternity to be renewed because the Holy Roman Emperor Frederick III was a member and petitioned the pope for approval. Unfortunately, due to wars, persecutions, and the burning of many Catholic libraries, especially those of the Dominicans, none of Bl. Alan's original manuscripts exist today.

Rosary Gems

The rosary in particular is a sign of predestination. Our fidelity in reciting it is a sure sign of salvation.

~ Blessed Alan de la Roche

All priests say a Hail Mary with the faithful before preaching, to ask for God's grace. They do this because of a revelation that Saint Dominic had from Our Lady. "My son," she said one day, "do not be surprised that your sermons fail to bear the results you had hoped for. You are trying to cultivate a piece of ground which has not had any rain. Now when Almighty God planned to renew the face of the earth, he started by sending down rain from heaven — and this was the Angelic Salutation. In this way God made over the world."

~ Blessed Alan de La Roche

One day when he [Blessed Alan] was saying Mass, Our Lord, who wished to spur him on to preach the holy rosary, spoke to him in the Sacred Host: "How can you crucify me again so soon?" Jesus said. "What did you say, Lord?" asked Blessed Alan, horrified. "You crucified me once before by your sins," answered Jesus, "and I would willingly be crucified again rather than have my Father offended by the sins you used to commit. You are crucifying me again now because you have all the learning and understanding that you need to preach my mother's rosary, and you are not doing so. If you only did this you could teach many souls the right path and lead them away from sin — but you are not doing it."

~ St. Louis de Montfort

Our Lady, too, spoke to him [Blessed Alan] one day to inspire him to preach the holy rosary more and more: "You were a great sinner in your youth," she said, "but I obtained the grace of your conversion from my Son. Had such a thing been possible I would have liked to have gone through all kinds of suffering to save you because converted sinners are a glory to me. And I would have done this also to make you worthy of preaching my rosary far and wide."

~ St. Louis de Montfort

Saint Dominic appeared to Blessed Alan as well and told him of the great results of his ministry: he [St. Dominic] had preached the holy rosary unceasingly, his sermons had borne great fruit and many people had been converted during his missions. He said to Blessed Alan: "See the wonderful results I have had through preaching the holy rosary! You and all those who love Our Lady ought to do the same so that, by means of this holy practice of the rosary, you may draw all people to the real science of the virtues."

~ St. Louis de Montfort

One day Our Lady said to Blessed Alan: "Just as Almighty God chose the Angelic Salutation to bring about the Incarnation of his Word and the redemption of mankind, in the same way those who want to bring about moral reforms and who want people reborn in Jesus Christ must honor me and greet me with the same salutation. I am the channel by which God came to men, and so, next to my son Jesus Christ, it is through me that men must obtain grace and virtue."

~ St. Louis de Montfort

One day Our Lady said to Blessed Alan: "I want people who have a devotion to my rosary to have my Son's grace and blessing during their lifetime and at their death, and after their death I want them to be freed from all slavery so that they will be like kings wearing crowns and with scepters in their hands and enjoying eternal glory."

~ St. Louis de Montfort

Our Lady also said to Blessed Alan: "I want you to know that, although there are numerous indulgences already attached to the recitation of my rosary, I shall add many more to every fifty Hail Marys (each group of five decades) for those who say them devoutly, on their knees — being, of course, free from mortal sin. And whosoever shall persevere in the devotion of the holy rosary, saying these prayers and meditations, shall be rewarded for it; I shall obtain for him full remission of the penalty and of the guilt of all his sins at the end of this life."

~ St. Louis de Montfort

One day Our Lord said to Blessed Alan: "If only these poor wretched sinners would say my rosary, they would share in the merits of my passion and I would be their Advocate and would appease my Father's justice."

~ St. Louis de Montfort

Blessed Alan said that a man he knew of had desperately tried all kinds of devotions to rid himself of the evil spirit who possessed him, but without success. Finally he thought of wearing the rosary around his neck, which eased him considerably. He discovered that whenever he took it off the devil tormented him cruelly, so he resolved to wear it night and day. This drove the evil spirit away forever, because he could not bear such a terrible chain. Blessed Alan also testified that he had delivered a large number of people who were possessed by putting the rosary around their necks.

~ St. Louis de Montfort

Blessed Alan says that he has seen several people delivered from Satan's bondage after taking up the holy rosary, even though they had previously sold themselves to him in body and soul by renouncing their baptismal vows and their allegiance to Our Lord Jesus Christ.

~ St. Louis de Montfort

Blessed Alan writes that many of the [Dominican] brethren had appeared to them while reciting the rosary, and had declared that next to the Holy Sacrifice of the Mass there was no more powerful means than the rosary to help the suffering souls [in purgatory]. Numerous souls were released daily who otherwise would have been obliged to remain in purgatory for years.

~ St. Alphonsus Liguori

Blessed Alan relates the story of a noble lady of Aragon named Alexandra, who had been the cause of jealousy and hatred among several young men of her city. As a result of this rivalry, she was killed, and her body cast into a well. St. Dominic, who had converted her, recommended her to the Confraternity of the Holy Rosary, and himself said many prayers to Mary for the repose of the lady Alexandra's soul. The latter appeared to thank him in the name of the souls who were suffering in purgatory with her, and to beg him to preach everywhere the practice of the rosary in suffrage, because they enjoyed the greatest relief through it.

~ Blessed James Alberione

May he [St. Joseph] obtain for us the ability of Father St. Dominic, St. Vincent Ferrer, and Blessed Alan de la Roche to promote the rosary.

~ Blessed Gabriele Allegra

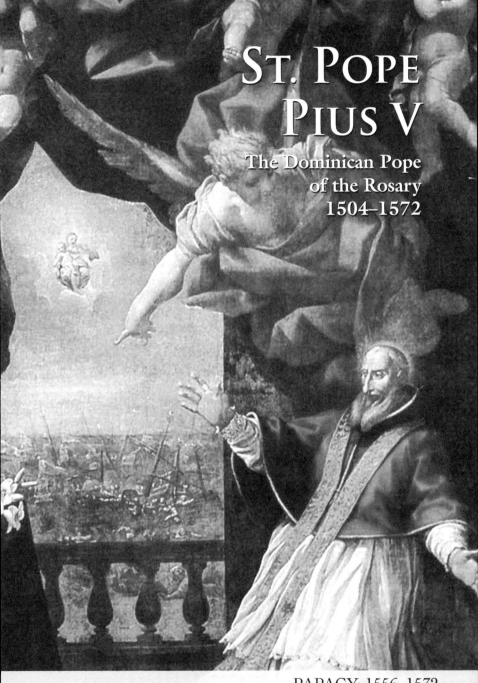

St. Pope Pius V

The Dominican Pope of the Rosary
1504–1572

PAPACY: 1556–1572
BEATIFIED: May 1, 1672 by Pope Clement X
CANONIZED: May 22, 1712 by Pope Clement XI
FEAST DAY: April 30

SAINT POPE PIUS V was 14 years old when he entered the Dominicans. A disciplined and learned man, Divine Providence elevated him to the papacy to be the "dog of God" who would bark against the Protestant rebellion and attack the Islamic Turks who desired to conquer Christianity and Western Civilization. As a reforming pontiff, he was very zealous in reforming the laxity of the clergy as well as the moral corruption of many in the hierarchy. He is responsible for the successful implementation of the decrees of the Council of Trent and the standardization of the liturgy. Though extremely busy as the Vicar of Christ, he remained very devoted to his religious order and wore his white Dominican habit under his papal attire. According to most historians, he set the precedent for all subsequent popes to wear a white cassock as part of their papal attire.

Marian Devotion

In his zeal for standardizing the liturgy, St. Pope Pius V revised the Divine Office (Liturgy of the Hours) in 1568. As part of the revision, he inserted the complete version of the Hail Mary prayer (already in use in other breviaries) into the universal Roman Breviary. This action officially established the complete Hail Mary prayer — the exact version we pray today — as the universally approved formula. The complete version of the Hail Mary did not originate with the pontificate of St. Pope Pius V, since it had been in use since the 14th century, but to his perpetual honor and credit, he established it as the universal norm.

In response to the Protestant rebellion, St. Pope Pius V issued the *Catechism of the Council of Trent*. This catechism included the official Church teachings on the Virgin Mary. As a friend of St. Charles Borromeo, the reforming cardinal and bishop of Milan, St. Pope Pius V was very supportive of Borromeo's efforts to champion the rosary against the Protestants. He especially supported Borromeo's defense of Catholicism by emphasizing the necessary role of the Virgin Mary in the life of Christ and the Church. Saint Pope Pius V is buried in the greatest Marian church of the Catholic world, the Basilica of Santa Maria Maggiore in Rome.

Champion of the Rosary

Saint Pope Pius V was one of the greatest papal champions of the rosary. He authored two extraordinary documents on the rosary, promoted the rosary as *the* means of conquering Islam, and established a liturgical feast in honor of the rosary. His first document on the rosary, titled *Consueverunt Romani Pontifices,* was promulgated on September 17, 1569. Along with praising the rosary, this apostolic letter contains many statements affirming the pious tradition and encourages the frequent recitation of the rosary, especially in response to ongoing threats from the Muslims.

In response to the threat of invasion from the Ottoman Turks (Muslims), St. Pope Pius V formed a Holy League, an army to beat back the forces of Islam. Knowing the power of the rosary, he intentionally established the Holy League on the Feast of St. Dominic. As part of his efforts to defeat the Muslims, he asked Christians throughout the world, especially in Italy, to pray for victory over the Muslims by gathering together and praying the rosary. He himself gathered people together in Rome at the Dominican church of Santa Maria Sopra Minerva and prayed the rosary for this intention. His prayers and the prayers of all the faithful were heard. As historical records attest, before news had reached Rome that the Muslims had been defeated at the Battle of Lepanto, St. Pius V had already received a vision in which he saw Our Lady and knew with certainty that the battle had been won by the Holy League.

In gratitude for the victory at Lepanto, and convinced that the victory had come through the rosary campaign he had initiated, he promulgated his second rosary document, *Salvatoris Domini,* on March 15, 1572. In this document, he directed that a feast be celebrated every year on October 7 as a commemoration of the victory over the Muslims. The feast was appropriately titled Our Lady of Victory. In the same document, in order to give special recognition to the role the rosary played in the Battle of Lepanto, he also established Rosary Sunday. This annual liturgical celebration was to be held on the first Sunday of October, and those who participated in the celebrations were granted a plenary indulgence. He also granted a plenary indulgence to anyone who joined the Confraternity of the Rosary.

Rosary Gems

[Saint] Dominic invented this method of prayer, which is easy and suitable to everyone and which is called the Rosary or the Psalter of the Blessed Virgin Mary. It consists of venerating this Blessed Virgin by reciting 150 Angelic Salutations, the same number as the Psalms of David, interrupting them at each decade by the Lord's Prayer, meanwhile meditating on the mysteries which recall the entire life of our Lord Jesus Christ.

~ St. Pope Pius V

After having devised it [the rosary], Dominic and his sons [the Dominicans] spread this form of prayer throughout the Church. The faithful welcomed it with fervor, were soon set on fire by this meditation and were transformed into other men; the darkness of heresy receded; the light of the faith reappeared, and the Friars of the same Order, legitimately commissioned by their Superiors, founded associations of the rosary everywhere, in which the faithful had themselves enrolled.

~ St. Pope Pius V

This devotion [the rosary], which reverently honors both the principal mysteries of Christ and her who alone has crushed every heresy of the 13th century and later on, often defeated the enemies of the Church. Rightly, therefore, we must hope that the same power [of the rosary] will repulse the errors of hell, will annihilate the machinations of godlessness, will remove from the people the errors that have been propagated and, with it, the great upheaval that convulses all mankind.

~ St. Pope Pius V

By the rosary the darkness of heresy has been dispelled, and the light of the Catholic Faith shines out in all its brilliancy.

~ St. Pope Pius V

Inspired by the Holy Ghost, as is piously believed, Blessed Dominic, Founder of the Order of Friar-Preachers, in a time like the present, when France was infested by the Albigensian heresy, which had blinded so many followers of this world that they raved against the priests of the Lord, raising his eyes to heaven, and seeking some easy and good method of prayer to God, which should be within the reach of all, devised the Rosary or Psalter of the Blessed Virgin.

~ St. Pope Pius V

Saint Pius V, one of the greatest Popes who ever ruled the Church, said the rosary every day.

~ St. Louis de Montfort

It is said that the Pontiff [St. Pius V] knew by Divine Revelation of the victory of Lepanto achieved at that very moment when through the Catholic world the pious sodalities of the holy rosary implored the aid of Mary in that formula initiated by the Founder of the Friar Preachers and diffused far and wide by his followers.

~ Pope Benedict XV

In the 16th century, the archenemy [the Turks] threatened all the port cities of the Mediterranean with its terrible fleet. Pius V brought together an armada in union with Spain, Venice, and the Knights of Malta, with Don Juan as admiral. Pius himself, a second Moses, set himself at the head of a storm of prayer. At his word, the rosary was prayed by all Christianity in order to secure Mary's favor in the decisive battle upon which the fate of Italy and all Europe depended.

~ Servant of God Joseph Kentenich

St. Louis de Montfort

The Preacher of the Rosary
1673–1716

BEATIFIED: January 22, 1888 by Pope Leo XIII
CANONIZED: July 20, 1947 by Venerable Pope Pius XII
FEAST DAY: April 28

SAINT LOUIS DE MONTFORT was born in Brittany in 1673. As a zealous preacher of the eternal wisdom of Jesus Christ, the Cross, and the Virgin Mary, he walked over 18,000 miles on foot all throughout Europe in the course of his evangelization efforts. In 1706, Pope Clement XI confirmed the fruitfulness of his preaching ministry and commissioned him to be an apostolic missionary. He founded two religious communities: the Missionaries of the Company of Mary (Montfort Fathers) and the Daughters of Wisdom. He conducted missions at over 200 parishes and authored many books that are acclaimed as classics of Catholic theology and spirituality. On one occasion while preaching, he punched and knocked out several intoxicated hecklers because they were mocking the subject of his message, namely, Jesus and Mary. Saint Louis de Montfort was a force to be reckoned with! He died at age 43 and was buried in Saint-Laurent-sur-Sèvre, France, in the basilica named after him. He was canonized in 1947.

Marian Devotion

Saint Louis de Montfort is one of the greatest Marian saints of all time, if not *the* greatest. His most famous work on Our Lady is the Marian masterpiece *True Devotion to the Blessed Virgin*. For 126 years, it lay hidden in a chest buried in a field until it was re-discovered in 1842. After it was found and published, it quickly became *the* primary Mariological work referenced by all subsequent Marian saints, scholars, and popes. *True Devotion to the Blessed Virgin* has been published in over 300 editions and translated into more than 20 languages. Saint Louis de Montfort is known as *the* saint of Marian consecration. He also authored the very popular book *The Secret of Mary*.

The Marian devotion of St. Louis de Montfort is superlative. Synthesizing the Marian teachings of the first 17 centuries of the Church, he preached and wrote about Mary as the "Lady of breathless beauty," the masterpiece of God's creation, and the surest and most effective way to truly follow Jesus Christ. There have been few saints who have so beautifully and succinctly expressed the essence of Marian devotion as St. Louis de Montfort. He taught that as the Mother of God and the spiritual mother of

God's children, Mary is the aqueduct and Mediatrix of All Grace, the heart of the Mystical Body of Christ, the air we breathe, the quickest and easiest way to Jesus, and the mold of saints. As the mold for creaturely holiness, Mary is understood by St. Louis to be the ultimate saint-maker and thus a necessary mediatrix in our sanctification. For anyone who desires to go deeper into Marian devotion and piety, there is no substitute for reading the original works of St. Louis de Montfort. In God's time, St. Louis de Montfort's Marian genius may well be cause for the Church to declare him a Doctor of the Church.

Champion of the Rosary

Saint Louis de Montfort is the author of the greatest book ever written on the rosary, *The Secret of the Rosary*. Similar to *True Devotion*, it was unknown during his lifetime and only re-discovered in the mid-19th century. Since it was first published in 1911, millions and millions of copies have been made and countless translations undertaken. Through *The Secret of the Rosary*, the Church and the world were once again made aware of the importance of the rosary in the lives of St. Dominic and Bl. Alan de la Roche. Saint Louis de Montfort titled his book *The Secret of the Rosary* because so few souls truly know the secret of sanctity that is contained and hidden in the blessed beads of Our Lady. There is no other book that gives so much honor to the rosary. Its author can truly be said to be an apostle, a champion, and the greatest writer on the rosary in the history of the Church.

Saint Louis de Montfort loved the rosary so much that he became a Third Order Dominican on November 10, 1710. He obtained permission from the Master General of the Order of Preachers to preach the rosary everywhere he went and established confraternities of the rosary during his missions. It is estimated that he enrolled over 100,000 people in the Confraternity of the Rosary during his lifetime. He especially recommended the rosary to priests as a means of converting as many souls as possible and taught that the rosary offers grace in this life and glory in the next. Just as St. Dominic used the rosary to overcome the Albigensians in the 13th century, so did St. Louis use the rosary to preach against the Jansenists in the 18th century. As an apostolic missionary and a Third Order Dominican, he wore a 15-decade rosary from his belt as a spiritual sword. The practice of including the Apostles' Creed, the initial Our Father, and three Hail Marys at the beginning of the rosary, as well as assigning a fruit to each mystery, is attributed to his preaching.

Rosary Gems

This [the rosary] is one of the greatest secrets to have come down from heaven.

~ St. Louis de Montfort

It would hardly be possible for me to put into words how much Our Lady thinks of the holy rosary and of how she vastly prefers it to all other devotions.

~ St. Louis de Montfort

Almighty God has given it [the rosary] to you because he wants you to use it as a means to convert the most hardened sinners and the most obstinate heretics. He has attached to it grace in this life and glory in the next.

~ St. Louis de Montfort

When the Holy Spirit has revealed this secret [of the rosary] to a priest and director of souls, how blessed is that priest! If a priest really understands this secret he will say the rosary every day and will encourage others to say it.

~ St. Louis de Montfort

Let all men, the learned and the ignorant, the just and the sinners, the great and the small praise and honor Jesus and Mary, night and day, by saying the most holy rosary.

~ St. Louis de Montfort

I beg of you to beware of thinking of the rosary as something of little importance — as do ignorant people and even several great but proud scholars. Far from being insignificant, the rosary is a priceless treasure which is inspired by God.

~ St. Louis de Montfort

Since the holy rosary is composed, principally and in substance, of the prayer of Christ and the Angelic Salutation, that is, the Our Father and the Hail Mary, it was without doubt the first prayer and the first devotion of the faithful and has been in use all through the centuries, from the time of the apostles and disciples down to the present.

~ St. Louis de Montfort

When people say the rosary together it is far more formidable to the devil than one said privately, because in this public prayer it is an army that is attacking him. He can often overcome the prayer of an individual, but if this prayer is joined to that of other Christians, the devil has much more trouble in getting the best of it. It is very easy to break a single stick, but if you join it to others to make a bundle it cannot be broken.

~ St. Louis de Montfort

Our Lady has shown her thorough approval of the name Rosary; she has revealed to several people that each time they say a Hail Mary they are giving her a beautiful rose and that each complete rosary makes her a crown of roses.

~ St. Louis de Montfort

The rose is the queen of flowers, and so the rosary is the rose of all devotions and it is therefore the most important one.

~ St. Louis de Montfort

Nobody can condemn devotion to the holy rosary without condemning all that is most holy in the Catholic Faith, such as the Lord's Prayer, the Angelic Salutation and the mysteries of the life, death and glory of Jesus Christ and of his holy Mother.

~ St. Louis de Montfort

I promise you that if you practice this devotion and help to spread it you will learn more from the rosary than from any spiritual book.

~ St. Louis de Montfort

Never will anyone who says his rosary every day become a formal heretic or be led astray by the devil. This is a statement that I would gladly sign with my blood.

~ St. Louis de Montfort

Arm yourselves with the arms of God — with the holy rosary — and you will crush the devil's head and you will stand firm in the face of all his temptations. This is why even the material rosary itself is such a terrible thing for the devil, and why the saints have used it to enchain devils and to chase them out of the bodies of people who were possessed.

~ St. Louis de Montfort

It must not be thought that the rosary is only for women and for simple and ignorant people; it is also for men and for the greatest of men.

~ St. Louis de Montfort

Please do not scorn this beautiful and heavenly tree, but plant it with your hands in the garden of your soul, making the resolution to say your rosary every day.

~ St. Louis de Montfort

Somebody who says his rosary alone only gains the merit of one rosary, but if he says it together with thirty other people he gains the merit of thirty rosaries. This is the law of public prayer. How profitable, how advantageous this is!

~ St. Louis de Montfort

If a church or a chapel is not available, say the rosary together in your own or a neighbor's house.

~ St. Louis de Montfort

If you say the rosary faithfully until death, I do assure you that, in spite of the gravity of your sins you shall receive a never fading crown of glory. Even if you are on the brink of damnation, even if you have one foot in hell, even if you have sold your soul to the devil as sorcerers do who practice black magic, and even if you are a heretic as obstinate as a devil, sooner or later you will be converted and will amend your life and save your soul, if — and mark well what I say — if you say the holy rosary devoutly every day until death for the purpose of knowing the truth and obtaining contrition and pardon for your sins.

~ St. Louis de Montfort

To become perfect, say a rosary a day.

~ St. Louis de Montfort

True servants of the Blessed Virgin, like Dominic of old, will range far and wide, with the holy Gospel issuing from their mouths like a bright and burning flame, and the rosary in their hands, and being like your watchdogs, burn like fire and dispel the darkness of the world like a sun.

~ St. Louis de Montfort

ST. ALPHONSUS LIGUORI

The Doctor of the Rosary
1696–1787

BEATIFIED: September 15, 1816 by Pope Pius VII
CANONIZED: May 26, 1839 by Pope Gregory XVI
DOCTOR OF THE CHURCH: March 23, 1871
by Bl. Pope Pius IX
FEAST DAY: August 1

SAINT ALPHONSUS LIGUORI was born near Naples and lived to be 90 years old. Gifted with an incredible intellect, he obtained a doctorate in law from the University of Naples at the age of 16. After many years practicing law, he abandoned his law practice, studied to become a priest, and quickly became one of the greatest moral theologians in the history of the Church. He authored a mammoth collection of theological and devotional writings, penning more than 100 publications. During his lifetime, he was consecrated a bishop, founded the Congregation of the Most Holy Redeemer (Redemptorists), and was a major promoter of frequent visits to the Blessed Sacrament.

Marian Devotion

From his youth, St. Alphonsus had a pious and filial love toward the Virgin Mary. He learned much of his Marian devotion from his devout and saintly mother. On the day of the conferral of his doctorate degree — at the age of 16 — he knelt down before the entire faculty of the University of Naples and professed a solemn oath to defend the truth of Mary's Immaculate Conception. In his day, this truth was not defended by all Catholics because the dogma of the Immaculate Conception would not be defined until 1854. Throughout his life and priestly ministry, he always promoted and defended the Immaculate Conception of Mary in all of his Marian writings. After his death, heaven rewarded his efforts to promote the Immaculate Conception. In 1871, he was declared a Doctor of the Church by the same pope, Bl. Pope Pius IX, who proclaimed the dogma of the Immaculate Conception in 1854.

The story of how St. Alphonsus responded to the call from God to become a priest manifests his unmistakable Marian character. When he gave up his legal practice and decided to become a priest, he went to the statue of Our Lady of Mercy in the Church of Our Lady of Ransom in Naples, knelt down, took off his cavalier's sword and placed it at the feet of the statue of Mary. This action symbolized that he no longer desired to be a servant of the mundane, but a servant and knight of the Queen of Heaven. He fasted every Saturday in honor of Our Lady. As a priest and theologian, he became one of the most important

Marian authors of the 18th century. His Marian influence on clergy and laity alike was tremendous. He often preached on the notion that Mary was a new Noah's ark in which sinners could find refuge from the storms of life.

In 1750, he published his Marian masterpiece, *The Glories of Mary*. This book took him 16 years to write. Because St. Louis de Montfort's books were not discovered until 1842, *The Glories of Mary* had a head start, and so has the privilege of being the most widely distributed Marian book of all time. It has gone through over 800 editions and been translated into dozens of languages. Though he had no knowledge of the Marian works of St. Louis de Montfort, *The Glories of Mary* has many similarities to the works of St. Louis de Montfort and was likewise meant to counter the Jansenism of his day. Like St. Alphonsus had done with all of his books, it was written in front of an image of Our Lady of Good Counsel that the saint kept on his desk. In the opening paragraphs of *The Glories of Mary*, he states that he owes everything to Mary and notes that it is his great desire to spread devotion to her. He taught that Mary's mantle serves as a protective cloak for sinners and, after the honor we owe Jesus Christ, we are to give chief place in our hearts to the love of Mary, our spiritual mother. He composed hymns to Mary, painted images of her, and wrote a commentary on the *Salve Regina*. He was so well loved by the pope that he was consecrated a bishop at the Dominican Church of Santa Maria Sopra Minerva in Rome in 1762. He died as the *Angelus* was being prayed, holding an image of Mary in his hands.

Champion of the Rosary

As a Doctor of the Church, St. Alphonsus is sometimes also referred to as the "Doctor of Prayer." One of the prayers he prayed every day was the rosary. He was so devoted to the rosary that, toward the end of his life when his memory was slowly fading, he often expressed concern to those around him if he was uncertain that he had prayed his rosary on that particular day. The rosary was his daily companion till the end.

It is truly amazing to think that St. Alphonsus lived in the same century as St. Louis de Montfort, but did not know of the existence of *The Secret of the Rosary*. Yet St. Alphonsus proved himself to be a true champion of the rosary by both his life and *The Glories of Mary*. In his book, he gave many examples of the power of the rosary in the lives of those who prayed it, even providing stories of people who were miraculously saved through the power of the rosary. He himself encouraged people to join the Confraternity of the Rosary and emphasized that people should pray the rosary to help the souls in purgatory. To this day, a 15-decade rosary is part of the religious habit of the Redemptorists.

Rosary Gems

There is no devotion so generally practiced by the faithful of all classes as that of the rosary.

~ St. Alphonsus Liguori

The rosary should be said with devotion.

~ St. Alphonsus Liguori

It is well to say the rosary kneeling, before an image of Mary, and, before each decade, to make an act of love to Jesus and Mary, and ask them for some particular grace.

~ St. Alphonsus Liguori

The immense good that this noble devotion [the rosary] has done to the world is well known. How many, by its means, have been delivered from sin! How many led to a holy life! How many to a good death, and are now saved!

~ St. Alphonsus Liguori

In an earthquake a poor woman was buried under the ruins of a house which was overthrown. A priest had the stones and rubbish cleared away, and under them found the mother with her children in her arms, alive and uninjured. On being asked what devotion she had practiced, she replied, that she never omitted saying the rosary, and visiting the altar of our Blessed Lady.

~ St. Alphonsus Liguori

A person who was leading an immoral life had not the courage to give it up; he began to say the rosary and was converted.

~ St. Alphonsus Liguori

A person who maintained a sinful friendship, by saying the rosary felt a horror of sin; she fell a few more times into sin, but by means of the rosary was soon quite converted.

~ St. Alphonsus Liguori

Saint Vincent Ferrer said to a man who was dying in despair, 'Why are you determined to lose your soul, when Jesus Christ wishes to save you?' The man answered that, in spite of Christ, he was determined to go to hell. The Saint replied, 'And you, in spite of yourself, shall be saved.' He [St. Vincent] began with the persons in the house to recite the rosary; when, behold, the sick man asked to make his confession; and having done so with many tears, expired.

~ St. Alphonsus Liguori

It is well known that the devotion of the most holy rosary was revealed to St. Dominic by the Blessed Mother herself, at a time when the saint was in affliction, and bewailing, with his Sovereign Lady, over the Albigensian heretics, who were at that time doing great mischief to the Church.

~ St. Alphonsus Liguori

If we want to help the souls in purgatory then we should say the rosary for them because the rosary gives them great relief.

~ St. Alphonsus Liguori

Suffice it to know that this devotion [the rosary] has been approved by the Church, and that the Sovereign Pontiffs have enriched it with indulgences.

~ St. Alphonsus Liguori

BLESSED POPE PIUS IX

The Servant of the Rosary
1792–1878

PAPACY: 1846–1878
BEATIFIED: September 3, 2000 by St. John Paul II
FEAST DAY: February 7

B LESSED POPE PIUS IX was pope for 31 years and
had the privilege of being the longest reigning pope in the
post-apostolic era of the Church. He suffered from epilepsy all
throughout his life. When he was a seminarian, he suffered such
an intense epileptic seizure that he was dismissed from both the
seminary and the Papal Noble Guard. It was only after he threw
himself at the feet of the Servant of God Pope Pius VII and
begged to be reinstated that the pope allowed him back into the
seminary and the Papal Noble Guard. During the first few years
of his priesthood, his health required that another priest assist him
during Mass due to his unpredictable seizures. Despite his epilepsy, he was made a bishop at the age of 35 and sent by the Pope
to Chile and Peru to assist the apostolic nuncio. Because of his
service in South America, he was the first man to hold the office
of the Vicar of Christ to have set foot in the Americas. When he
was elected to the papacy in 1846, he chose the name "Pius" in
honor of the Servant of God Pope Pius VII, since it was Pius VII
who had encouraged his vocation despite his epilepsy. He wrote
38 encyclicals, was the first pope to be photographed, and, at the
First Vatican Council, helped formulate the dogmatic definition
of papal infallibility.

Marian Devotion

Blessed Pope Pius IX is known as the "Pope of the Immaculate Conception." On December 8, 1854, it was his privilege
to dogmatically define Mary's Immaculate Conception. During
the official announcement of the new dogma, as he began to
pronounce the authoritative papal formula *declaramus* ("we
declare"), a beam of light descended into St. Peter's and shone
directly on him. Aware of the honor that was his in declaring
this dogma, he immediately began to cry and was so moved that
he had to cease reading the declaration until his tears subsided.
He truly loved the Immaculate Conception, and even before he
declared the dogma in 1854, had already given permission to the
bishops of the United States in 1847 to declare the Immaculate
Conception the patroness of the country.

In the writings of Bl. Pope Pius IX, Mary is described as
more holy than the cherubim and seraphim; all the tongues of

heaven and earth do not suffice to praise her as she truly deserves. As the mother of Jesus and our spiritual mother, her prayers have extraordinary power. God delights in answering her prayers since she serves as the Mediatrix of All Grace. To give the faithful a greater awareness of the importance of Mary's intercession, he instituted the Feast of Our Lady of Perpetual Help in 1876.

Champion of the Rosary

In 1858, during the pontificate of Bl. Pope Pius IX, heaven gave the Church a great gift when the Lourdes apparitions took place. Occurring only four years after the declaration of the dogma of the Immaculate Conception, the Lourdes apparitions brought about a renewed interest in the rosary. Throughout his pontificate, Bl. Pope Pius IX championed the rosary as a protection against vice and heresy, even stating that if he but had an army to pray the rosary, he could conquer the world! On May 7, 1867, he beatified the 205 martyrs of Japan, many of whom were Dominicans and members of the Confraternity of the Rosary.

As a result of the renewed interest in the rosary that emerged after the Lourdes apparitions, Bl. Pope Pius IX frequently preached on the rosary, wrote about it, and affirmed the plenary indulgence available to the faithful on Rosary Sunday. In 1868, at the request of Fr. Joseph Moran, a Spanish Dominican, Bl. Pope Pius IX granted an indulgence to all who attended October observances in honor of the rosary. The rosary was in the hands of this saintly pope to the very end of his life. At the age of 85, while he was praying the rosary with his staff, he died of a heart attack as the result of an epileptic seizure.

Rosary Gems

I could conquer the world if I had an army to say the rosary.

~ Blessed Pope Pius IX

Among all the devotions approved by the Church, none has been so favored by so many miracles as the rosary devotion.

~ Blessed Pope Pius IX

If you desire peace in your hearts, in your homes, in your country, assemble every evening to recite the rosary.

~ Blessed Pope Pius IX

The single richest treasure in the Vatican is the rosary.

~ Blessed Pope Pius IX

When St. Dominic, acting by the inspiration of God, had implored the help of the Immaculate Mother of our Lord to uproot the heresy of the Albigenses, and when he went forth to preach the rosary as a marvelous succor against heresy and sin, this devotion spread itself among the faithful in an admirable manner.

~ Blessed Pope Pius IX

As St. Dominic employed this prayer [the rosary] as a sword to destroy the monstrous heresy of the Albigenses, so likewise in our time the faithful, in using the same weapon — that is to say, the daily recitation of the rosary — will obtain that, by the all-powerful protection of the Mother of God, the many errors infecting the world will be uprooted and destroyed.

~ Blessed Pope Pius IX

Have courage, my dear children! I exhort you to fight against the persecution of the Church and against anarchy, not with the sword, but with the rosary.

~ Blessed Pope Pius IX

As you know, dear sons, it is a celebrated fact that the rosary was entrusted by the Holy Mother of God to St. Dominic as a singular help when he battled against monstrous errors.

~ Blessed Pope Pius IX

At the call and summons of God, St. Dominic, the founder of the Order of Friars Preachers, implored the help of the Immaculate Mother of God, to whom alone it appertains to destroy all heresies in the world, in order to overcome the errors of the Albigenses, and had begun to preach the rosary as a defense of marvelous power against heresies and vices.

~ Blessed Pope Pius IX

Let the rosary, this simple, beautiful method of prayer, enriched with many indulgences, be habitually recited in the evening in every household. These are my last words to you: the memorial I leave behind me.

~ Blessed Pope Pius IX

ST. ANTHONY MARY CLARET

The 'St. Dominic' of the Rosary
1807–1870

CATECHISMVS

BEATIFIED: February 25, 1934 by Pope Pius XI
CANONIZED: May 7, 1950 by Venerable Pope Pius XII
FEAST DAY: October 24

SAINT ANTHONY MARY CLARET was born in Sallent, Spain, and although he was only 5-foot-1 in height, he was a giant of the faith. As a young man, he desired to become a Carthusian monk, but due to poor health and the necessary rigors of eremitical life, he was turned away. He then thought of becoming a Jesuit and entered their novitiate, but after further discernment he left the Jesuits and ended up becoming a diocesan priest. He was very zealous in his priestly ministry, and even spent a year and a half preaching an extensive series of retreats in the Canary Islands. In his zeal for spreading the Gospel, he founded the Missionary Sons of the Immaculate Heart of Mary (Claretians) before being made the archbishop of Santiago, Cuba.

Saint Anthony helped bring about a great reform in the clergy and the Catholic Church in Cuba. He confirmed over 300,000 people, validated over 9,000 marriages, and sometimes preached as many as 12 sermons a day. It has been estimated that during his many years as a priest, he preached over 25,000 sermons! He also authored over 100 theological works. His efforts to bring about reform were not welcomed by everyone, however. The Freemasons in Cuba were particularly disturbed by his efforts, and several attempts were made on his life. During one assassination attempt, he was stabbed in the face. After his time in Cuba, he served as the confessor to the queen of Spain and helped with preparations for the First Vatican Council. He was a staunch defender of papal infallibility and helped formulate its definition at the Council. Due to failing health, he spent the last days of his life at a Cistercian monastery in France.

Marian Devotion

From his youth, St. Anthony had a tender devotion to the Blessed Virgin and frequently made visits to the Shrine of Our Lady of Fusimanya to pray the rosary with his sister Rosa. In his inspiring autobiography, he credits Our Lady with saving him on one occasion from drowning in treacherous waves, as well as helping him overcome a great temptation against purity. During a trip to Italy in 1839, for the first time he witnessed people exhibiting a great devotion to the Immaculate Heart of Mary. This helped him to develop a Marian devotion that would become known as the *cordimariana* ("Marian heart") spirituality. He was extremely devoted to the Immaculate Heart of Mary and, in 1847, founded the Archconfraternity of the Heart of Mary in Vic, Spain. Two years later, in 1849, he founded a religious community dedicated to the Immaculate Heart known as the Missionary Sons of the Immaculate Heart of Mary. When members of the community professed their religious vows, they were also required to make a solemn promise to propagate devotion to the Immaculate Heart of Mary.

Similar to St. Alphonsus Ligouri, St. Anthony understood Mary's Immaculate Heart to be a new Noah's ark. By entering her heart, mankind would be able to find a place of safety against the spiritual deluge overtaking the world. He also understood Mary's heart as the "mercy seat" from which all graces of the Holy Trinity are distributed. Saint Anthony's Marian theology was greatly influenced by the writings of St. Alphonsus Liguori. He often instructed people to read *The Glories of Mary*. Saint Anthony also loved the presentation of Mary in *The Mystical City of God* by Venerable Mary of Agreda. He himself wrote at least 10 works on the Virgin Mary. When he became a bishop, he inserted the name "Mary" into his own name. Before leaving for his diocese in Cuba, he made pilgrimages to three of his favorite Marian Shrines: the ones dedicated to Our Lady of Pilar, Our Lady of Montserrat, and Our Lady of Fusimanya. He lived during the era in which Bl. Pope Pius IX declared the dogma of the Immaculate Conception and Mary appeared to St. Bernadette at Lourdes.

Champion of the Rosary

When St. Anthony was very young, his parents gave him a rosary, enrolled him in the Confraternity of the Rosary, and offered him a great parental example by praying a daily rosary in the home. During his youth, he found a book on the rosary owned by his parents. After reading it, he became an ardent champion of the rosary all throughout his adolescence. Saint Anthony was so devoted to the rosary that he would frequently lead both children and adults in its recitation at the local parish. Immediately after becoming a seminarian, he joined the Perpetual Rosary Society and enrolled himself in the local Confraternity of the

Rosary. From the beginning of his seminary studies, he took up the practice of praying three rosaries a day, continuing this pious practice for the rest of his life. Once he became a priest, he rarely gave any sermon without having first instructed the people in how to pray the rosary. On many occasions, he would even pray a set of mysteries with everyone present before delivering his sermon.

Saint Anthony was consecrated a bishop on the Feast of Our Lady of the Rosary in 1850. There is sworn testimony from a man who was present at one of St. Anthony's Masses just a few days before his episcopal ordination that there were heavenly lights surrounding him as he offered Mass at a rosary altar. The young man who witnessed this event eventually became a priest and continued to tell others what he had seen during that Mass. As the archbishop of Santiago, Cuba, St. Anthony gave away over 20,000 rosaries and mandated that the rosary be prayed in all the churches in his diocese on Sundays and feast days. To make sure this practice was carried out, he often made surprise visits to parishes. He also authored several works on the rosary, translated a book on the rosary that had been written by another priest, and, in a book he wrote specifically for seminarians, insisted that every seminarian pray the rosary every day. Though he was completely unaware of St. Louis de Montfort's writings on the rosary and died seven years before Pope Leo XIII began writing rosary encyclicals, St. Anthony's explanation of the origins of the rosary are in perfect accord with *The Secret of the Rosary* and the 11 rosary encyclicals of Pope Leo XIII. Providentially, in 1899, one year after Pope Leo XIII wrote his last rosary encyclical, he declared Anthony Mary Claret a Venerable.

With such zeal for promoting the rosary, there is good reason why St. Anthony is acclaimed as the "St. Dominic" of the 19th century. A fellow Spaniard, he greatly loved St. Dominic, imitated him in his preaching-praying style, and always carried a rosary on his person. Of greater significance, however, is the fact that on several occasions, the Virgin Mary appeared to St. Anthony and informed him that he was to serve as the "St. Dominic" for the people of his time by zealously promoting the rosary.

Rosary Gems

When I was a little boy I was given a pair of rosary beads, and I was more pleased with them than with the greatest treasure.

~ St. Anthony Mary Claret

My parents, who are now in heaven, inspired in me a devotion to the holy rosary when I was still very young. They bought me a pair of beads and had me enrolled in the Confraternity of the Rosary in our parish.

~ St. Anthony Mary Claret

Before I had reached the age of reason I knelt daily to say a part of the rosary.

~ St. Anthony Mary Claret

Mother Mary, how good you have been to me and how ungrateful I have been to you! My mother, I wish to love you from now on with all my heart, and not only to love you myself, but to bring everyone else to know, love, serve, and praise you and to pray the holy rosary, a devotion that is so pleasing to you.

~ St. Anthony Mary Claret

On the ninth of the same month [October 9, 1857], at 4:00 in the morning, the Blessed Virgin Mary repeated several times what she had told me on other occasions — that I was to be the "Dominic of these times in spreading devotion to the rosary."

~ St. Anthony Mary Claret

Let victory be thine, O Mother. Thou wilt conquer. Yes, thou hast the power to overcome all heresies, errors, and vice. And I, confident in your powerful protection, will engage in the battle, not only against flesh and blood, but against the prince of darkness, as the Apostle [Paul] says, grasping the shield of the holy rosary and armed with the double-edged sword of the divine word.

~ St. Anthony Mary Claret

The good priest is not content with being a devotee of Mary, but rather he strives to promote every style of devotion to Mary; for example, teaching others to pray the rosary well.

~ St. Anthony Mary Claret

Have you said the rosary every day with devotion?

~ St. Anthony Mary Claret

Pray the rosary every day.

~ St. Anthony Mary Claret

We should meditate on the mysteries [of the rosary], applying them to the circumstances of our own lives.

~ St. Anthony Mary Claret

I found that another powerful means for doing good was giving away rosaries and teaching people how to use them.

~ St. Anthony Mary Claret

Mary Most Holy will be our Mistress, Directress, and Captainess, and we will be Brothers in the Brotherhood of Mary, Queen of the Rosary.

~ St. Anthony Mary Claret

The ancient peoples of the East had a practice of offering rose-wreaths to be worn as crowns to distinguished persons; and true Christians have the praiseworthy practice of offering each day with great devotion the crown of Marian roses to their beloved Mother, the Blessed Virgin. Such was the practice of St. Louis King of France, the great Bossuet, Fenelon, St. Vincent de Paul, St. Charles Borromeo, St. Francis de Sales, St. Francis Xavier, and others. Ever since the year 1208, during which the glorious St. Dominic taught people to pray it daily, there has not been a saint nor any person distinguished for learning and virtue, nor an observant religious community, nor a well-ordered seminary, which has not had the devotion to the rosary.

~ St. Anthony Mary Claret

It can be said that the rosary is a compendium of our holy religion.

~ St. Anthony Mary Claret

The holy rosary is comprised of many holy elements; no one doubts that this devotion is very pleasing to God and the holy Virgin. The devotion of the most holy rosary is powerful enough to transmit all graces and, as we are aware from experience, it has proven to be a remedy during times of war, plagues, hunger and other calamities; in addition, those who have been troubled in body or soul, if they had recourse to the rosary, always received consolation.

~ St. Anthony Mary Claret

The most holy rosary is an abundant mine through which Christians, praying and meditating with attention and devotion, become enriched with great merits.

~ St. Anthony Mary Claret

The rosary is a flower garden that contains all kinds of beautiful and aromatic virtues.

~ St. Anthony Mary Claret

The most holy rosary is the most powerful, easy, and gentle means for dispelling ignorance and for removing errors and heresies.

~ St. Anthony Mary Claret

The rosary is the strongest impulse of the human heart, and those who get hooked on it will improve their habits.

~ St. Anthony Mary Claret

Secular people who are well off and lacking in nothing often pray the holy rosary in the morning and the evening when traveling; how much more should seminarians and priests do likewise!

~ St. Anthony Mary Claret

Most Holy Virgin, obtain for us the grace to devoutly pray your most holy rosary.

~ St. Anthony Mary Claret

Long live the holy rosary of Mary!

~ St. Anthony Mary Claret

POPE LEO XIII

The Pope of the Rosary
1810–1903

PAPACY: 1878–1903

POPE LEO XIII is the longest lived pope in Church history, dying at 93. A brilliant writer, poet, and theologian, he established the Pontifical Academy of St. Thomas Aquinas in Rome in 1879 (now known as the Pontifical University of St. Thomas Aquinas, or the Angelicum). He was passionate about hunting and viniculture, and was known to trap birds and tend a small vineyard within the confines of the Vatican Gardens.

As a pastor of souls and a mystic, Pope Leo XIII was deeply concerned about the social and moral issues of his time, and gave the Church many spiritual weapons to combat these issues. While saying Mass one day, he had a vision of a fierce spiritual battle taking place and was inspired to write the famous Prayer to St. Michael the Archangel. He greatly promoted devotion to St. Joseph, consecrated the entire world to the Sacred Heart of Jesus, promoted the First Friday devotions, and established June as the month dedicated to the Sacred Heart. He is also the pope before whom a young Thérèse of Lisieux knelt, begging to be allowed to enter Carmel at the age of 15. He was the first pope to appear on film and beatified St. Louis de Montfort in 1888.

Marian Devotion

From his youth, Pope Leo XIII had a strong devotion to Mary. Through the discovery of the Marian writings of St. Louis de Montfort in 1846, and the subsequent investigations into these writings as part of de Montfort's beatification cause, Pope Leo XIII was deeply influenced by de Montfort's Marian thought. He was so enamored with *True Devotion to the Blessed Virgin* that he granted an indulgence to anyone who consecrated themselves to Mary using St. Louis de Montfort's method. Another source of Marian inspiration for Pope Leo XIII was the work of Blessed Bartolo Longo in Pompeii.

Pope Leo XIII was very open to private revelation. He promoted the Brown Scapular, instituted the Feast of Our Lady of the Miraculous Medal, wrote an apostolic letter promoting pilgrimages to Marian shrines, especially Lourdes, and received one of the visionaries of La Salette, Mélanie Calvat, in two separate private audiences. He so loved Lourdes that he commissioned the construction of a Lourdes Grotto in the Vatican Gardens.

Following the thought of St. Bernard of Clairvaux, he taught that a Christian trying to live their faith without Mary is comparable to a bird trying to fly without wings. In his many Marian writings, he emphasized that it is Our Lady who is capable of bringing about obedience to the Vicar of Christ among all Christians. He was the first pope to have his voice recorded; on the recording, he's singing the Hail Mary.

Champion of the Rosary

Pope Leo XIII is the greatest champion of the rosary to ever hold the office of the Vicar of Christ. During his pontificate, he wrote 11 encyclicals on the rosary, promulgated numerous apostolic letters on the rosary, and gave countless messages on the rosary to various dioceses and religious institutes. His rosary encyclicals contain a summary of all the statements previous popes had made about St. Dominic's role as the father of the rosary and the founder of the Confraternity of the Rosary. In almost every rosary encyclical that he wrote, he affirmed that St. Dominic was the founder of the rosary. He expressly taught that Our Lady herself entrusted the rosary to St. Dominic, and compared St. Dominic's Confraternity to an army of prayer and a spiritual battalion capable of winning souls for Christ.

A pontiff who sought to emphasize the importance of Catholic social teaching, he wrote the encyclical *Rerum Novarum* and also taught that the rosary was part of the solution to the social problems of his day. He tirelessly taught that the rosary was the most effective means of expanding the kingdom of Jesus Christ in the world and was of benefit to both individuals and society at large. He encouraged everyone to pray the rosary every day, and especially encouraged priests and missionaries to preach the rosary, since it has the power to expel evil and heal the sores of the human heart.

Pope Leo XIII dedicated the month of October to the rosary, granted many indulgences to the rosary, approved a comprehensive list of the indulgences attached to the rosary, affirmed Rosary Sunday, supported the construction of the Basilica of the Rosary in Lourdes, inserted the title "Queen of the Most Holy Rosary" into the Litany of Loreto, wrote a charter for the Confraternity of the Rosary, encouraged the Dominicans to promote the rosary, and supported the rosary apostolate of Bl. Bartolo Longo at the Basilica of the Rosary in Pompeii. Even a shortened version of his famous Prayer to St. Michael the Archangel is now commonly prayed at the end of the rosary. The writings of Pope Leo XIII highlighted a special blessing: To pray the rosary is to pray with the holy angels, since it was the Archangel Gabriel who uttered the first *Ave*. Pope Leo XIII will forever be *the* pope of the rosary.

Rosary Gems

It is mainly to expand the kingdom of Christ that we look to the rosary for the most effective help.

~ Pope Leo XIII

It is well known that there have been many persons occupied in most weighty functions or absorbed in laborious cares who have never omitted for a single day this pious practice. Combined with this advantage is that inward sentiment of devotion which attracts minds to the rosary, so that they love it as the intimate companion and faithful protector of life.

~ Pope Leo XIII

Experience has shown that to inculcate love for the Mother of God deeply in souls there is nothing more efficacious than the practice of the rosary.

~ Pope Leo XIII

In Mary, God has given us the most zealous guardian of Christian unity. There are, of course, more ways than one to win her protection by prayer, but as for us, we think that the best and most effective way to her favor lies in the rosary.

~ Pope Leo XIII

The rosary is the most excellent form of prayer and the most efficacious means of attaining eternal life. It is the remedy for all our evils, the root of all our blessings. There is no more excellent way of praying.

~ Pope Leo XIII

For every time we devoutly say the rosary in supplication before her, we are once more brought face to face with the marvel of our salvation; we watch the mysteries of our Redemption as though they were unfolding before our eyes; and as one follows another, Mary stands revealed at once as God's Mother and our Mother.

~ Pope Leo XIII

Meditation on the mysteries of the rosary, often repeated in the spirit of faith, cannot help but please her [Mary] and move her, the fondest of mothers, to show mercy to her children.

~ Pope Leo XIII

The rosary is by far the best prayer by which to plead before her [Mary] the cause of our separated brethren.

~ Pope Leo XIII

The formula of the rosary ... is excellently adapted to prayer in common, so that it has been styled, not without reason, "The Psalter of Mary." And that old custom of our forefathers ought to be preserved or else restored, according to which Christian families, whether in town or country, were religiously wont at close of day, when their labors were at an end, to assemble before a figure of Our Lady and alternately recite the rosary. She, delighted at this faithful and unanimous homage, was ever near them like a loving mother surrounded by her children, distributing to them the blessings of domestic peace, the foretaste of the peace of heaven.

~ Pope Leo XIII

For in the rosary all the part that Mary took as our co-Redemptress comes to us.

~ Pope Leo XIII

The rosary, if rightly considered, will be found to have in itself special virtues, whether for producing and continuing a state of recollection, or for touching the conscience for its healing, or for lifting up the soul.

~ Pope Leo XIII

May Mary, the Mother of God and of men, herself the authoress and teacher of the rosary, procure for us its happy fulfillment.

~ Pope Leo XIII

The spirit of prayer and the practice of Christian life are best attained through the devotion of the rosary of Mary.

~ Pope Leo XIII

In places, families, and nations in which the rosary of Mary retains its ancient honor, the loss of faith through ignorance and vicious error need not be feared.

~ Pope Leo XIII

The rosary of the Blessed Virgin Mary, combining in a convenient and practical form an unexcelled form of prayer, an instrument well adapted to preserve the faith and an illustrious example of perfect virtue, should be often in the hands of the true Christian and be devoutly recited and meditated upon.

~ Pope Leo XIII

The Blessed Virgin alone can save us, and she will renew the wonders of Lepanto.

~ Pope Leo XIII

The origin of this form of prayer [the rosary] is divine rather than human.

~ Pope Leo XIII

They [Confraternities of the Rosary] are, so to speak, the battalions who fight the battle of Christ, armed with his sacred mysteries, and under the banner and guidance of the heavenly Queen.

~ Pope Leo XIII

We may well believe that the Queen of Heaven herself has granted an especial efficacy to this mode of supplication [the rosary], for it was by her command and counsel that the devotion was begun and spread abroad by the holy Patriarch Dominic as a most potent weapon against the enemies of the faith at an epoch not, indeed, unlike our own, of great danger to our holy religion.

~ Pope Leo XIII

Pope Sixtus V, of happy memory, approved the ancient custom of reciting the rosary; Gregory XIII dedicated a day under this title, which Clement VIII afterward inscribed in the Martyrology, and Clement XI extended to the Universal Church. Benedict XIII inserted the feast in the Roman Breviary, and we ourselves, in perpetual testimony of our affection for this devotion, commanded that the solemnity with its office should be celebrated in the Universal Church.

~ Pope Leo XIII

Let all the children of Saint Dominic rise up for the fight and let them, like mighty warriors, be prepared to use in the battle the weapons with which their blessed Father, with so much foresight, armed them. This is what they have to do: Let them plant everywhere the rosary of the Blessed Virgin Mary; let them propagate and cultivate it with fervor; through their assiduous care may the nations be enrolled in these holy militias where the ensigns of the rosary shine; may the faithful learn to avail themselves of this weapon, to use it frequently; may they be instructed in the benefits, graces, and privileges of this devotion.

~ Pope Leo XIII

In the darkness of the times, Leo XIII appeared like a new dawn, and if he diffused much light in the universe through his great genius and indefatigable work, it cannot be denied that everything in him was the fruit of his devotion and love for the Blessed Virgin. He wrote eleven encyclicals on the rosary and enriched this prayer with indulgences.

~ Blessed James Alberione

During a most trying time for the Church, when for a long time a dreadful tempest of evils had been oppressing us, Leo XIII, in a series of encyclical letters, strongly urged the faithful all over the world to recite the holy rosary frequently.

~ Blessed James Alberione

The [rosary] encyclicals [of Pope Leo XIII] had varied contents, but they were all very wise, vibrant with fresh inspiration, and directly relevant to the practice of the Christian life. In strong and persuasive terms they exhorted Catholics to pray to God in a spirit of faith through the intercession of Mary, his Virgin Mother, by reciting the holy rosary.

~ St. Pope John XXIII

Blessed Bartolo Longo

The Apostle of the Rosary
1841–1926

BEATIFIED: October 26, 1980 by St. John Paul II
FEAST DAY: October 5

B LESSED BARTOLO LONGO was born near Naples, Italy, to a devout Catholic family that prayed the rosary. As a young man, he studied law at the University of Naples. After being swept away by various political ideologies, he became anti-Catholic, radically opposed to what he believed were the "old wives' tales" of Catholicism. He particularly disdained the papacy, the priesthood, and the Dominicans. His hatred for the Dominicans was, in part, due to his disdain for their intellectual and academic efforts to defend Catholicism against the secular philosophies Bartolo had embraced. Within a short period of time, he went from adhering to nationalistic ideologies to becoming involved in spiritualism. This led him to attend séances and become an ordained priest of Satan.

Bartolo's involvement with the occult and spiritualism left him empty and unhappy. He suffered from hallucinations, torturous nightmares, frazzled nerves, bodily ailments, and severe depression. Seeking guidance, he turned to a friend and a Dominican priest, and began to experience a radical conversion. Fearing for his soul, he renounced spiritualism and its practices, and turned back to the Catholicism of his youth. In gratitude for having been delivered from the occult, he became a Third Order Dominican and dedicated his life to the spread of the rosary, especially by renewing the Catholic faith in the ancient city of Pompeii and building there the Basilica of Our Lady of the Rosary. He initiated many charitable works as part of his apostolate and was made a knight of the Order of the Holy Sepulchre.

Marian Devotion

Though he turned away from Catholicism during his legal studies in Naples, Bartolo always maintained a reverence for the feminine mystery and treated all women with respect and dignity. His respect for women stemmed from his love for his earthly mother. It was this mother-son bond that God used to bring about his radical conversion through Mary, his spiritual mother. In fact, when he abandoned spiritualism, he set out to make unparalleled efforts to cause Mary to be better known and loved. Our Lady became the Queen of his heart and his great hope of finding salvation in Christ. He relied completely upon her in all his works and efforts to help souls.

When St. John Paul II beatified Bl. Bartolo in 1980, he offered the following thoughts in his homily on Bl. Bartolo's great Marian devotion: "Bartolo Longo, a Third Order Dominican, and founder of the religious institution 'The Daughters of the Most Holy Rosary of Pompeii,' can truly be defined as 'the man of the Virgin': for love of Mary he became a writer, apostle of the Gospel, propagator of the rosary, founder of the famous sanctuary [of the rosary] in the midst of enormous difficulties and adversities; for love of Mary he created charitable institutions, became a beggar for the children of the poor, transformed the city of Pompeii into a citadel of human and Christian goodness; for love of Mary he silently endured calumny and tribulations, passing through a long Gethsemane, always trusting in Providence, always obedient to the Pope and the Church."

Champion of the Rosary

After his reversion back to Catholicism, Bl. Bartolo became a Third Order Dominican on October 7, 1871, and took the name "Br. Rosario," a name whose importance may not have been completely clear to him at that time. The rosary would come to be his anchor and hope of salvation when, during a work-related visit to Pompeii in 1872, he underwent a great challenge to his faith.

During the trip, he discovered that the people living near the ancient city of Pompeii were suffering from a severe lack of catechesis and had succumbed to the errors of spiritualism. Seeing the failing state of Pompeii caused him to go into a severe depression, since he knew that he had once been a priest of Satan, leading many people away from the faith and into the falsehoods of spiritualism. He felt as if he was still under the bondage of the devil, and a deep sense of hopelessness came over him so strongly that he contemplated suicide. There was only one thing that drew him out of his depression: calling to mind Mary's promise to St. Dominic that whoever promotes the rosary will be saved. Relying on this promise, he put away his suicidal intentions and gave his life entirely over to the promotion of the rosary. He began to incorporate the rosary into everything he did. Every evening, he would gather with others to pray the rosary in common in church. The rosary became the sweet chain that bound him to Jesus and Mary, and broke the bondage of Satan.

The promotion of the rosary and the restoration of the Catholic faith in Pompeii became Bartolo's mission in life. In 1873, he began a confraternity in Pompeii, and, inspired by his friend St. Caterina Volpicielli and her work of spreading devotion to the Sacred Heart of Jesus in Naples, he began the construction of a Shrine dedicated to Our Lady of the Rosary in Pompeii. As he was furnishing his rosary shrine, he obtained an image of Our Lady of the Rosary and had it restored. Through this image, God worked miracles so that the whole world would come to believe in the power of the rosary.

In 1877, he published *The Fifteen Saturdays*, a book about miracles associated with the rosary. In 1884, he launched a magazine dedicated to the rosary (still in circulation today) called *Il Rosario e la Nuova Pompeii* (*The Rosary and the New Pompeii*). He became a friend of St. Joseph Moscati, a saintly physician from Naples who prayed the rosary every day. Saint Moscati came to know Bl. Bartolo through serving as his personal physician and grew to love the Shrine of Our Lady of the Rosary of Pompeii. On average, 4 million people visit the Shrine of Our Lady of the Rosary of Pompeii every year. Saint John Paul II, Pope Benedict XVI, and Pope Francis have all made personal pilgrimages to the Basilica of the Rosary in Pompeii to pray and encourage others to pray the rosary. Blessed Bartolo Longo was buried on the Feast of Our Lady of the Rosary (October 7, 1926). In *Rosarium Virginis Mariae*, St. John Paul II's letter on the rosary, he gave Bl. Bartolo the title "the apostle of the rosary."

Rosary Gems

My only purpose in thirty-three years of service has been that of saving my soul and that of my brother by spreading the most holy rosary.

~ Blessed Bartolo Longo

The rosary is a teacher of life, a teacher full of gentleness and love, where people beneath the gaze of Mary, almost without noticing, discover they are being slowly educated in preparation for the second life, that which is authentic life, for it is not destined to end in a very few years, but to go unto eternity.

~ Blessed Bartolo Longo

Just as two friends, frequently in each other's company, tend to develop similar habits, so too, by holding familiar converse with Jesus and the Blessed Virgin, by meditating on the mysteries of the rosary and by living the same life in Holy Communion, we can become, to the extent of our lowliness, similar to them and can learn from these supreme models a life of humility, poverty, hiddenness, patience and perfection.

~ Blessed Bartolo Longo

The rosary, in a gentle, subtle way leads one to the Eucharist, to the Most Blessed Sacrament: those who approach Jesus in thought, yearn to approach him in reality; those who know Jesus cannot but love him; indeed, those who truly love Jesus cannot forego possessing him.

~ Blessed Bartolo Longo

The rosary could very well be called the poem of human redemption. The rosary is a poem that takes its lively but simplistic hues from the pure palette of the Gospel; while at the same time it draws its logical ties, its harmonious responses, its entire intimate dialectic from the highest theology.

~ Blessed Bartolo Longo

If it be true that you [Mary] promised St. Dominic that whoever spreads the rosary will be saved, I will be saved, because I shall not depart from this land of Pompeii without having spread your rosary.

~ Blessed Bartolo Longo

Sweet Queen of my heart, kindly accept the prayer I address to you, that your love may spread in my heart and in the hearts of all those who honor you by reciting the rosary.

~ Blessed Bartolo Longo

Awaken your confidence in the Most Holy Virgin of the Rosary!

~ Blessed Bartolo Longo

O Blessed Rosary of Mary, sweet chain which binds us to God, bond of love which unites us to the angels, tower of salvation against the assaults of hell, safe port in our universal shipwreck, we shall never abandon you.

~ Blessed Bartolo Longo

I thought that perhaps as the priesthood of Christ is for eternity, so also the priesthood of Satan is for eternity. So, despite my repentance, I thought that I was still consecrated to Satan, and that I am still his slave and property as he awaits me in Hell. As I pondered over my condition, I experienced a deep sense of despair and almost committed suicide. Then I heard an echo in my ear of the voice of Friar Alberto repeating the words of the Blessed Virgin Mary: "One who propagates my rosary shall be saved."

~ Blessed Bartolo Longo

My God, you did not look at my past, you did not stop before my weakness; in one hand you placed the rosary, in the other a pen, and you said to me: "Write, they will listen to you, for it is I who will place in your heart the word of life."

~ Blessed Bartolo Longo

You [Mary] are omnipotent by grace and therefore you can help us. Were you not willing to help us, since we are ungrateful children and undeserving of your protection, we would not know to whom to turn. Your motherly heart would not permit you to see us, your children, lost. The Infant whom we see on your knees and the blessed rosary which we see in your hand inspire confidence in us that we shall be heard.

~ Blessed Bartolo Longo

The rosary is a seat, upon which Mary sits as teacher, to teach us the way by which we can attain life.

~ Blessed Bartolo Longo

Bartolo Longo, a Third Order Dominican, and founder of the religious institution "The Daughters of the Most Holy Rosary of Pompeii," can truly be defined as "the man of the Virgin": for love of Mary he became a writer, apostle of the Gospel, propagator of the rosary, founder of the famous sanctuary in the midst of enormous difficulties and adversities; for love of Mary he created charitable institutions, became a beggar for the children of the poor, transformed the city of Pompeii into a citadel of human and Christian goodness; for love of Mary he silently endured calumny and tribulations, passing through a long Gethsemane, always trusting in Providence, always obedient to the Pope and the Church.

~ St. John Paul II

Bartolo Longo is the apostle of the rosary, the layman who fully lived his Christian commitment.

~ St. John Paul II

When we see, in the famous painting of Our Lady of Pompeii, the Virgin Mother and the Child Jesus giving the rosary beads to St. Catherine of Siena and St. Dominic, we immediately understand that this prayer leads us through Mary to Jesus, as Pope John Paul II taught us in his letter Rosarium Virginis Mariae, *in which he explicitly mentions Bl. Bartolo Longo and the charism of Pompeii.*

~ Pope Benedict XVI

I am pleased to emphasize that like St. Paul, Bartolo Longo was transformed from persecutor to apostle: an apostle of Christian faith, of Marian devotion and, in particular, of the rosary, in which he found a synthesis of the whole Gospel.

~ Pope Benedict XVI

SERVANT OF GOD
JOSEPH
KENTENICH

The Friend of the Rosary
1885–1968

THE SERVANT OF GOD JOSEPH KENTENICH was born near Cologne, Germany, in 1885, and joined the Pallotines in 1904. As a spiritual director and teacher at the Pallottine seminary in Schoenstatt, Germany, he was inspired to found the Schoenstatt movement in 1914. The Schoenstatt movement is essentially an education movement with a very strong Marian dimension. As an educator of youth and a zealous promoter of the Catholic apostolate, Fr. Kentenich sought to bring about a spiritual, moral, and anthropological renewal in the world through Mary.

In 1941, during World War II, Fr. Kentenich was arrested by the Gestapo and put into prison. In 1942, due to medical reasons, he was given the opportunity to avoid time in a concentration camp, but he made a resolution to offer up his suffering for the Schoenstatt movement. He spent three years in Dachau. His suffering for the movement proved very fruitful, and continued even after he was freed.

Father Kentenich's apostolic work was ahead of his time and would only be fully appreciated after the Second Vatican Council. During his lifetime, his intentions were often misunderstood. At one point, he was forced to surrender control of the Schoenstatt movement to others and was transferred to a Pallottine house in Milwaukee, Wisconsin. Before he left for the United States, he made a pilgrimage to the shrine of Our Lady of the Rosary of Pompeii to entrust everything to Mary. During his time on administrative leave in Wisconsin, he had nothing to do with Schoenstatt for 14 years (1951-1965). Unfortunately, during his exile in Wisconsin, he was the subject of unfounded suspicions and was stripped of his faculties to offer Mass publicly for one week. Blessed Pope Paul VI ended Kentenich's exile in 1965, and he was able to return to Germany. Once he returned to Europe, he left the Pallotines and became a diocesan priest. He died on September 15, 1968 (the Feast of Our Lady of Sorrows). On his tomb are the words *Dilexit Ecclesiam* ("He loved the Church"). That is all he wanted written on his grave.

Marian Devotion

When he was nine, Kentenich's mother had to make the difficult decision to leave her son at the orphanage of St. Vincent in Oberhausen, Germany, because she was unable to care for him. Before a statue in the orphanage that depicted Our Lady giving the rosary to St. Dominic and St. Catherine of Siena, his mother consecrated him to Mary and begged the Blessed Virgin to educate her son and be his mother. This event made a lasting impression on the young boy. Throughout his life, he uttered the famous Pallottine phrase *Mater habebit curam* ("Mother takes care") in reference to the maternal assistance of the Blessed Virgin.

Through learning and living the Marian spirituality of the Pallottine community, Kentenich came to understand Our Lady as the great missionary, educator, and teacher. As a novice, he read *True Devotion to the Blessed Virgin* by St. Louis de Montfort and was greatly influenced by it. As a seminarian, he thoroughly studied de Montfort's works and, once ordained, he preached many conferences on the Montfortian method of Marian consecration. He was a zealous promoter of the Marian Sodality. On October 18, 1914, during his talk to the Marian sodality at the minor seminary in Schoenstatt, he asked Our Lady to erect her throne in that place in a special way. This event marked the beginning of the Schoenstatt movement. In the same year, 1914, he also read an article about the zealous apostolic work of Bl. Bartolo Longo in Pompeii and was strongly inspired to turn Schoenstatt into an international movement.

The special characteristic of the Schoenstatt Marian movement is the covenant of love the members make with the Mother Thrice Admirable, giving her a blank check, which means that Mary can do with them whatever she desires. The Schoenstatt form of Marian consecration is lived out by the members loving, imitating, and invoking Mary, as well as by the various apostolic works that they undertake. All members of the movement are called to be apparitions of Mary in the world and lead people closer to Jesus by being an *altera Maria* ("another Mary"). Father Kentenich compared the members of Schoenstatt to the star of the Magi, leading people to Jesus and Mary. In the brilliant mind of Fr. Kentenich, the Marian dogmas of the Church were understood to be a compendium of all the great truths of Catholicism. His anthropological Mariology was a precursor to St. John Paul II's theology of the body. Father Kentenich perceived Mary to be the most beautiful bait that God uses to catch human hearts and bring them back to Christ. Mary, in essence, is a magnet for souls, and God desires to draw her triumphal chariot onto the battlefield of today's crisis-filled era in order to obtain peace and the restoration of all things in Christ.

Champion of the Rosary

Spending three years in the concentration camp of Dachau gave Fr. Kentenich a keen sense of the very real and ongoing spiritual battle between good and evil. He understood Mary to be the great Victress in this battle over all demons and heresies, and always insisted that the rosary is our friend in this battle. The rosary is the choice weapon that Mary gives to her soldiers and knights on the battlefield. A man of his times, Fr. Kentenich compared the rosary to an atomic bomb, noting that the rosary is much more powerful than even the greatest of man-made bombs. He taught that a child of Mary has nothing to fear on the battlefield since she is the victorious Queen and triumphant Mother of God. He would often boldly proclaim: *Servus Mariae Nunquam Peribit!* ("A Servant of Mary will never perish!").

Father Kentenich taught that Mary is our great educator and her classroom is the rosary. By means of the rosary, she teaches her children to avoid anything and everything that brings sadness to our heavenly Father. The rosary is not only our friend in times of battle, but also in times of joy, since it helps us avoid sin. In 1950, in order to advance a new effort of evangelization through the rosary, an apostolate known as the Schoenstatt Rosary Campaign began in Brazil. It spread quickly and, by 1976, extended to other countries in South America. In 1985, for the celebrations taking place to mark the centennial of Fr. Kentenich's birth, the Schoenstatt Rosary Campaign was launched on a global scale and began to spread all throughout the world.

Rosary Gems

The great remedy of modern times which will influence the events of the world more than all diplomatic endeavors and which has a greater effect on public life than all organizational ones, is the rosary.

~ Servant of God Joseph Kentenich

In the Middle Ages the Cathar sect [adherents to the Albigensian heresy] spread like wildfire. Kings fought to destroy it. It was overcome by the rosary.

~ Servant of God Joseph Kentenich

The Hail Marys [of the rosary] transport us into the sacred space of Mary's heart.

~ Servant of God Joseph Kentenich

The rosary is a sort of machine gun and atomic bomb, namely a weapon that is far superior to all the weapons of modern warfare in overcoming the enemy of God.

~ Servant of God Joseph Kentenich

The rosary has proven itself as a friend in the life and work of great men.

~ Servant of God Joseph Kentenich

The rosary is a good friend in joy, but an even better friend in battle. Today the drums continuously beat for battle. Our lives are one big battle. We are dependent on loyal, good friends. The rosary is such a good friend in the big battle of our time.

~ Servant of God Joseph Kentenich

The rosary is our good friend. Being familiar with it configures us to Christ. Through the rosary we become apparitions of Christ and encounters of Christ. How important a good friend is! A friend gives a child a sense of being sheltered even in a strange place. A good friend is a great treasure and a great rarity. Oh, the beautiful things that have been said and sung about friendship! And we may say and sing all this of the rosary, our good friend!

~ Servant of God Joseph Kentenich

What fruits the world and the Church owe to the rosary!

~ Servant of God Joseph Kentenich

Those who pray the rosary do more for the benefit of the whole human race than all the orators and deputies, more than all the organizers, secretaries and writers, more than all the capitalists even if they would make their entire wealth available to the Church.

~ Servant of God Joseph Kentenich

Let us immerse ourselves into the ocean of love which the rosary allows us to drink in richly, and let the glowing love of Christ and his Mother inflame our weak sacrificial spirit.

~ Servant of God Joseph Kentenich

SERVANT OF GOD LÚCIA DOS SANTOS

The Visionary
of the Rosary
1907–2005

THE SERVANT OF GOD LÚCIA DOS SANTOS was born in Aljustrel, Portugal, in 1907, and lived to be 97 years old. On May 13, 1917, the Blessed Virgin Mary began appearing to little Lúcia and two of her cousins, Jacinta and Francisco Marto, in the nearby village of Fatima. With one exception, Mary appeared to the three little children on the thirteenth of the month from May to October. (In August, Mary appeared a few days later, since the children had been put in jail.) During the last apparition on October 13, 1917, the famous Miracle of the Sun occurred. During that apparition, the sun gyrated and danced across the sky; more than 70,000 people witnessed it. The messages of Fatima contain many themes, most of which are centered on making reparation to the Immaculate Heart of Mary, doing penance, praying for peace, Marian consecration, and the rosary.

Shortly after the apparitions, Lúcia's two cousins, Jacinta and Francisco, died. Lúcia herself went on to become a Sister of St. Dorothy and then a Discalced Carmelite nun. Jacinta and Francisco were beatified on April 9, 2000, by St. John Paul II, and canonized on May 13, 2017, by Pope Francis. Sister Lúcia was a friend of St. John Paul II and met with him on several occasions. She wrote six memoirs of her life, recounting her experiences of Our Lady and the Fatima messages. When she died on February 13, 2005, Portugal declared a national day of mourning two days later.

Marian Devotion

After the Marian apparitions occurred in Fatima, Sr. Lúcia received several other visitations from Mary during her years in the Dorothean convent in Pontevedra, Spain. During the apparition of December 10, 1925, Our Lady revealed to Sr. Lúcia her desire for the Five First Saturdays devotion in reparation to her Immaculate Heart. With a special mission and vocation to make reparation to the Sacred Heart of Jesus and the Immaculate Heart of Mary, Sr. Lúcia sought to spread devotion to Mary's Immaculate Heart through her memoirs.

When Sr. Lúcia became a cloistered Carmelite nun, she was able to enter into a more prayerful and intense Eucharistic life. Sister Lúcia viewed Mary as the first monstrance that revealed Jesus to the nations. (The word "monstrance" stems from the Latin word *monstrare,* which means "to show.") In her writings, Sr. Lúcia emphasized that Mary is also the living tabernacle of the presence of Jesus Christ. The entire work of our redemption started in Mary's Immaculate Heart.

Champion of the Rosary

When Sr. Lúcia was a young girl, her family prayed a daily rosary together during the month of May every year. Lúcia was considered to be mature and pious for her age and so was allowed to receive her First Holy Communion at the age of six, even though the normal age for that special occasion was 10. After receiving the Eucharist for the first time, she knelt down and prayed before a statue of Our Lady of the Rosary, and later testified that the statue smiled at her.

During the Fatima apparitions, Mary stressed the importance of the recitation of the rosary. All three children became champions of the rosary and encouraged others to pray it with them before each apparition. Little Francisco became so zealous in praying the rosary that, during one of the apparitions, he told Our Lady that he would pray as many rosaries as she wanted. Later in life, when Sr. Lúcia recorded her memories, she frequently mentioned the great fervor that Sts. Jacinta and Francisco had for the rosary.

Mary also specifically asked Sr. Lúcia to learn how to read and write so that she could communicate to the world the importance of the rosary and the messages Mary was giving her. Our Lady particularly emphasized the daily rosary as a means of bringing about an end to World War I. Mary also revealed to the children a new prayer that she wanted to be added at the end of each decade of the rosary. The prayer was, "Oh my Jesus, forgive us our sins, save us from the fires of hell, and lead all souls to heaven, especially those most in need of thy mercy." Since Sts. Jacinta and Francisco died shortly after the apparitions, it was Sr. Lúcia who made this prayer more widely known. In essence, the Fatima apparitions were rosary apparitions; Mary confirmed this when, on October 13, the day of the last apparition and the day the Sun danced, Mary revealed to the children that she was Our Lady of the Rosary.

After the Fatima apparitions, Our Lady continued to instruct Sr. Lúcia on the importance of the rosary. During the apparition on December 10, 1925, in Pontevedra, Spain, Mary taught Sr. Lúcia the Five First Saturdays Devotion. An essential aspect of this devotion is that souls are to pray the rosary and spend at least 15 minutes meditating on the mysteries. Sister Lúcia understood the rosary and various forms of devotion associated with it to be concrete ways that all people could co-operate with Jesus, our Redeemer, and Mary, our Co-Redemptrix. She showed this specifically when, during Lent, she would pray the Chaplet of the Five Wounds with her arms outstretched! (The Chaplet of the Five Wounds originated with the Passionists in the early 19th century.) She considered the rosary to be a type of spiritual nourishment and made rosaries to give away to little children. In one of her memoirs, she also wrote beautiful meditations for the mysteries of the rosary.

Rosary Gems

My daughter [Sr. Lúcia], look at my heart surrounded with the thorns with which ungrateful men pierce it at every moment by their blasphemies and ingratitude. You, at least, try to console me, and say that I promise to assist at the hour of death with all the graces necessary for salvation all those who, on the first Saturday of five consecutive months, go to Confession and receive Holy Communion, recite five decades of the rosary and keep me company for a quarter of an hour while meditating on the mysteries of the rosary, with the intention of making reparation to me.

~ Our Lady to the Servant of God Lúcia Dos Santos

At the end of the rosary, she [St. Jacinta Marto] always said three Hail Marys for the Holy Father.

~ Servant of God Lúcia Dos Santos

The rosary is the prayer which God, through his Church and Our Lady, has recommended most insistently to us all, as a road to and gateway of salvation.

~ Servant of God Lúcia Dos Santos

During the month of May, we used to recite the rosary as a family every day.

~ Servant of God Lúcia Dos Santos

When lovers are together, they spend hours and hours repeating the same thing: "I love you!" What is missing in the people who think the rosary monotonous is Love; and everything that is not done for love is worthless.

~ Servant of God Lúcia Dos Santos

The prayer of the rosary, after the Holy Liturgy of the Eucharist, is what most unites us with God by the richness of [the] prayers that compose it. All of them [the prayers of the rosary] came from heaven, dictated by the Father, by the Son, and by the Holy Spirit. The "Glory" we pray between the decades was dictated by the Father to the angels when he sent them to sing it close to his Word, the newborn child. It is also a hymn to the Trinity. The "Our Father" was dictated by the Son and it is a prayer to the Father. The "Hail Mary" is all impregnated with Trinitarian and Eucharistic sense. The first words were dictated by the Father to the angel when he sent him to announce the mystery of the incarnation of the Word. Moved by the Holy Spirit, Saint Elizabeth said: "Blessed are thou amongst women, and blessed is the fruit of thy womb." The Church also moved by the Holy Spirit, added, "Holy Mary, Mother of God, pray for us sinners now and at the hour of our death."

~ Servant of God Lúcia Dos Santos

The Most Holy Virgin, in these last times in which we live, has given a new efficacy to the recitation of the rosary to such an extent that there is no problem, no matter how difficult it is, whether temporal or above all spiritual, in the personal life of each one of us, of our families ... that cannot be solved by the rosary. There is no problem, I tell you, no matter how difficult it is, that we cannot resolve by the prayer of the holy rosary.

~ Servant of God Lúcia Dos Santos

All well-intentioned people can, and should, recite the five decades of the rosary every day. The rosary should constitute each person's spiritual food.

~ Servant of God Lúcia Dos Santos

Our Lady insists that we pray the rosary every day because she knows our inconstancy, our weakness and our need.

~ Servant of God Lúcia Dos Santos

God, who is our Father and understands better than we do the needs of his children, chose to stoop to the simple ordinary level of all of us in asking for the daily recitation of the rosary, in order to smooth for us the way to him.

~ Servant of God Lúcia Dos Santos

Those who say the rosary daily are like children who, every day, manage to find a few moments just to be with their father, to keep him company, to show him their gratitude, to do some service for him, to receive his advice and blessing. It is an exchange of love, the love of the father for the child and the child for the father; it is a mutual giving.

~ Servant of God Lúcia Dos Santos

After the Holy Liturgy of the Eucharist, the prayer of the rosary is what better draws to our spirit the mysteries of Faith, Hope and Charity. She [the rosary] is the spiritual bread of souls.

~ Servant of God Lúcia Dos Santos

The rosary is the prayer of the poor and the rich, of the wise and the ignorant. To uproot this devotion from souls, is like depriving them of their daily spiritual bread. She [the rosary] is what supports that little flame of faith that has not yet been completely extinguished from many consciences. Even for those souls who pray without meditating, the simple act of taking the beads to pray is already a remembrance of God, of the supernatural.

~ Servant of God Lúcia Dos Santos

The simple remembrance of the mysteries in each decade is another radiance of light supporting the smoking torch of souls. This is why the devil has moved against it such a great war. And the worst part is that he has deluded and deceived souls of great responsibility by their position [on the rosary]. They are blind men leading blind men. They pretend to base their saying [on the rosary] in the [Second Vatican] Council and do not realize that the Holy Council ordered them to preserve all the practices that in course of years had been fostered in honor of the Immaculate Virgin Mother of God. The prayer of the rosary is one of the most important and, according to the decrees of the Holy Council and the orders of the Holy Father, it must be maintained.

~ Servant of God Lúcia Dos Santos

I will pray the rosary every day. For this I must go to the chapel a quarter of an hour before the ringing [of the bell] for Mass and pray the first rosary, meditating on the joyful mysteries. At four o'clock in the afternoon when I am usually alone, I will make a visit to Jesus present in the Blessed Sacrament and pray the second rosary, meditating on the sorrowful mysteries. Then if I have time, I will do the Stations of the Cross. If at this time I cannot, I will do it after the examination of the night. The third rosary I recite with the community at 6:30 pm, and I will meditate on the glorious mysteries.

~ Servant of God Lúcia Dos Santos

There are those who say that the rosary is an antiquated and monotonous prayer because of the constant repetition of the prayers which compose it. But I put the question: Is there anything kept alive without the perseverance in the continual repetition of some actions?

~ Servant of God Lúcia Dos Santos

The holy rosary, according to Lúcia of Fatima, is so powerful that it can solve any problem, material or spiritual, national or international.

~ Blessed Gabriele Allegra

St. Maximilian Kolbe

The Knight of the Rosary
1894–1941

BEATIFIED: October 17, 1971 by Bl. Pope Paul VI
CANONIZED: October 10, 1982 by St. John Paul II
FEAST DAY: August 14

SAINT MAXIMILIAN KOLBE was born in Zdunska Wola, Poland, and became a Conventual Franciscan. At a very young age he earned doctorates in both philosophy and theology from pontifical universities in Rome. During his studies in Rome, he was greatly disturbed when he witnessed protests against the Church and the papacy by Freemasons. His response to these protests was to establish the Militia Immaculatae (MI) in 1917, the same year that the Fatima apparitions occurred. The MI was founded to be a Marian movement to counter the Freemasons and the Modernists infiltrating the Church.

Saint Maximilian was on fire with zeal for serving Christ and his Church through apostolic works and even conducted missionary work in the Far East, especially in Japan. In Nagasaki, he established a religious house that would later experience miraculous protection during the atomic bombing of Nagasaki on August 9, 1945. Back in Europe, during World War II, St. Maximilian was arrested by the Gestapo and sent to the Nazi concentration camp of Auschwitz. In a heroic act of selfless Christian charity, he volunteered to die in the place of a total stranger, Franciszek Gajowniczek, since this man had a family. The intention of the Nazis was to kill St. Maximilian and everyone in his cell through starvation. However, after two weeks, St. Maximilian had outlived all the other prisoners, and the Nazis killed him by means of an injection of carbolic acid. His body was cremated at the concentration camp on August 15, 1941, the Feast of the Assumption of Mary into heaven. For his heroic love, the Church has declared him a martyr of charity. When Maximilian was beatified in 1971 and canonized in 1982, Franciszek Gajowniczek, the man whose life he had saved, was in attendance during the ceremonies.

Marian Devotion

As a young boy, St. Maximilian often expressed a desire to be a soldier. In 1906, after an episode in which his mother asked him what would become of him, he had a vision of Mary in which she offered him two crowns: one crown was white and represented purity; the other crown was red and represented martyrdom. Our Lady asked him which he desired, and, in his soldier-like zeal, he exclaimed that he wanted both! From that moment, his devotion to Mary was like that of a medieval knight for his fair lady. Saint Maximilian helped to re-introduce Marian chivalry into the hearts of many Catholics. In the Kolbe home, the family had an altar dedicated to Our Lady of Czestochowa, the Queen of Poland, where he would spend long hours in prayer before the image of his queen.

Shortly after he joined the Conventual Franciscans, he was sent to Rome to study. It was in Rome that he first heard about the miraculous conversion of Alphonse Ratisbonne. Ratisbonne was a Jewish man who received a vision of Mary in 1842 that ultimately led to his conversion to Catholicism, becoming a great promoter of the Miraculous Medal, and ordination as a Jesuit priest. This story inspired in St. Maximilian a desire to use the Miraculous Medal as a means of praying for the conversion of the enemies of the Church, especially the Freemasons and the Modernists. In preparation for founding the MI, he studied the Miraculous Medal apparitions given to St. Catherine Labouré, focusing especially on the promises that Mary made to St. Catherine regarding the medal. He so believed in the power of the Miraculous Medal that, when he founded the MI, he required each member to wear one. Then, once he was ordained a priest, he celebrated his first Mass at the altar of Our Lady in the Church of Sant'Andrea della Fratte in Rome, at the exact spot where Alphonse Ratisbonne had received his vision of Mary. Throughout St. Maximilian's whole life as a priest, he used the Miraculous Medal as a spiritual weapon, referring to it as a spiritual bullet against the enemies of Christ.

In 1927, he founded a monastery in Poland known as the City of the Immaculate (Niepokalanów), sometimes also called Marytown. It quickly became the center of an intense Marian apostolate, including a radio station and publication house that produced literature on Our Lady. At one point, the monastery housed almost 900 friars! Saint John Paul II visited Niepokalanów in 1983.

Saint Maximilian also founded a very popular magazine titled the *Knight of the Immaculate*. In 1930, as a missionary in Japan, he established a mission house in Nagasaki called the Garden of the Immaculate. As a Franciscan, he had a tremendous love for the Immaculate Conception and personalized the title by referring to Our Lady as the "Immaculata." Because of his zeal for the Immaculata, he had a special love for Lourdes since Mary had revealed herself to St. Bernadette as the Immaculate Conception.

Synthesizing the Catholic tradition on Marian consecration and, like nearly every other promoter of consecration to Jesus through Mary, heavily influenced by St. Louis de Montfort, St. Maximilian developed his own formula for Marian consecration. He believed that those who give their lives completely to Mary are to be her docile instruments in bringing about the "marianization" of all things in Christ. Drawing from the Franciscan tradition of Marian thought, he also emphasized Our Lady's role as the Spouse of the Holy Spirit, even stating that she is the quasi-incarnation of the Holy Spirit. He went so far as to say that the true purpose of a follower of Christ is to be "transubstantiated" into the Immaculate. This "transubstantiation" means that all followers of Christ are to become another Mary in their essence, that is, sinless, pure, holy, and immaculate. Saint Maximilian truly desired to win all souls for Christ through the Immaculate Co-Redemptrix and Mediatrix of All Grace.

Champion of the Rosary

Saint Maximilian was a true knight of the rosary and prayed it every day of his priestly life. Though he intended the Miraculous Medal to be the primary weapon of the Militia Immaculatae, he also required that all members pray the rosary every day. He preached and spoke frequently of the power of the rosary, taught his friars about the history of the rosary, and offered a kind of catechesis on the mysteries associated with the rosary. As a knight of the Immaculata, he understood the rosary to be a spiritual sword, and explicitly noted that each Knight and Lady of the Immaculate (members of the Militia Immaculatae) were to wield it with devotion and fervor.

In 1941, when he was captured by the Nazis and sent off to the concentration camp, one of the Nazi officers noticed the rosary hanging from his habit and used it as a means to abuse him. The Nazi officer violently grabbed the rosary, held up the crucifix to the saint's face, and asked him if he truly believed in Jesus Christ and the rosary. Saint Maximilian's response was "yes," for which he was brutally beaten several times in front of all the other prisoners. As a prisoner in Auschwitz, St. Maximilian frequently led the other prisoners in praying the rosary, especially those who shared his cell. Saint Maximilian is both a martyr of charity and a knight of the rosary.

Rosary Gems

The origin of the rosary is well known. A contemporary witness [of St. Dominic], Fr. Tiery of Alpola [Fr. Theodoric of Apolda lived from 1228–1297], a Dominican, recounts it. He says that St. Dominic could not in a particular locality convert the heretics; he turned to the Blessed Virgin Mary, whom he had highly revered since his childhood, and asked for assistance. The Queen of Heaven then appeared to him, showed him the rosary, and instructed him to propagate it. He fervently set to work, and from that time he recovered with ease a great many souls who had strayed, so that soon their number exceeded one hundred thousand. The whole Catholic world eagerly received the holy rosary, and innumerable graces and miracles of conversion testified to its supernatural origin.

~ St. Maximilian Kolbe

The popes have highly recommended it [the rosary], and as [Pope] Hadrian VI asserts: "the rosary defeats Satan." [Pope] Paul III said, "Through the rosary of St. Dominic, God's wrath toward France and Italy was restrained," and [Pope] Julius III proclaims, "The rosary is the ornament of the Roman Church." [Pope] Gregory XIV: "The rosary is the eradication of sin, the recovery of grace, the increase of God's glory." [Pope] Paul V: "The rosary is a treasure of graces." [Pope] Urban VIII: "Through the rosary, the number of most fervent Christians increases." [Blessed Pope] Pius IX: "If you desire peace to reign in your hearts and families, gather together each evening to recite the rosary." Pope Leo XIII in his encyclical on the rosary says, "We strongly urge all the faithful, whether it be publicly in the churches or in private homes and within the family, to pray the rosary and, as far as possible, not to relent in this holy exercise."

~ St. Maximilian Kolbe

In addition to the Lord's Prayer and the Angelic Salutation the essence of the rosary is contemplating the mysteries of the life of Christ the Lord and the most holy Mother of God.

~ St. Maximilian Kolbe

The scapular, the rosary, and the Miraculous Medal: here are three things that the Immaculata herself deigned to offer for the salvation of mankind.

~ St. Maximilian Kolbe

Knights and Ladies of the Immaculata, and all of you who read these words ... recite a third part [five decades] of the rosary daily.

~ St. Maximilian Kolbe

It is true that one is not under pain of sin in regard to praying the rosary — but what kind of love would ours be if it were limited to our strict obligations, neglect of which would be a serious transgression? Such conduct would appear more as the service of a slave than the love of a child towards his best Father in heaven, and most affectionate Mother. No! This is unworthy of a lover of Mary. Such a person seeks rather the opportunity to go to her as often as possible, to remain at her feet as long as possible.

~ St. Maximilian Kolbe

Can a pagan recite the rosary? And why not? Indeed, in that case, he may delve more easily into the truth of our faith. By praying, he may obtain the grace to know the truth in religious matters and the strength to accept such religion much more easily. He will acknowledge it as true, regardless of setbacks or judgments from others who are still unfamiliar with matters of faith.

~ St. Maximilian Kolbe

It [the rosary] is so easy to understand that children, and also simple persons who do not know how to read, can use the rosary as a means to prayer.

~ St. Maximilian Kolbe

One has to have great patience and trust in her. Moreover, one must pray much in times of trouble and suffering. One needs to invoke her most sweet name, "Mary," or say a "Hail Mary," and in the most difficult and most crucial times it will not hurt to even recite a whole section of the rosary.

~ St. Maximilian Kolbe

A prayer both simple and sublime that the Immaculata herself indicated when she appeared in Lourdes is the holy rosary. May it become the sword of each knight of the Immaculata, just as the Miraculous Medal is the bullet that strikes down evil!

~ St. Maximilian Kolbe

May the Miraculous Medal be the bullet in the hand of the Knights of the Immaculata and the holy rosary the sword.

~ St. Maximilian Kolbe

Prayer, therefore, and especially the rosary and penance — here are the Immaculata's orders for us all.

~ St. Maximilian Kolbe

The head of all the varied members of the infernal dragon is undoubtedly in our times — Freemasonry. And she shall crush his head. Further, history teaches us that there was hardly a conversion in which Mary's hand was not particularly seen. All the saints fostered a special devotion to her, and the Holy Father, Leo XIII says in an encyclical on the rosary (September 22, 1891), "It can be affirmed that from the immense treasure of all grace ... nothing is given to us by the will of God, except through Mary, and as no one can approach the Most High Father but by the Son, so ordinarily no one can approach Christ but by his mother."

~ St. Maximilian Kolbe

In October, Catholics have the custom of venerating the Most Holy Mother by reciting the rosary in churches or in private homes, and even the Immaculata, manifesting herself at Lourdes in 1858, appeared with rosary in hand, thus encouraging us by her own example to recite it. We therefore surely give great pleasure to the Mother of God and draw down upon ourselves and our families many blessings from God when we recite the rosary.

~ St. Maximilian Kolbe

In her apparition at Lourdes, in 1858, the Mother of God held in her arms the rosary, and through [St.] Bernadette, recommended to us the recital of the rosary. We can conclude, therefore, that the prayer of the rosary makes the Immaculata happy. Moreover, with this prayer we can easily obtain great graces and divine blessing.

~ St. Maximilian Kolbe

Behold, if we desire to rise even to her [Mary's] knowledge and loving of Jesus, we must whisper "Hail Mary," and repeating it, meditate upon these mysteries [of the rosary] in union with her.

~ St. Maximilian Kolbe

In every Catholic home, even the poorest, it is possible to find a rosary. Above all, in the hour of prayer, in church, or during a funeral, one notices that the faithful keep in their hands a rosary. In moments of joy or sadness, whenever the faithful turn to God in prayer, they recite the rosary and are deeply bonded with it.

~ St. Maximilian Kolbe

The humble prayer to the Immaculata, the holy rosary, together with heartfelt prayers, will indicate when and how to act, because in those moments it is she who directs, in those moments it is she who erases any difficulty.

~ St. Maximilian Kolbe

There is often mention of fifteen promises, by means of which the Most Blessed Virgin exhorts the faithful to recite the rosary. Those who received these promises were St. Dominic and Bl. Alan de la Roche.

~ St. Maximilian Kolbe

SERVANT OF GOD
FRANK DUFF

The Man of the Rosary
1889–1980

THE SERVANT OF GOD FRANK DUFF was born into a wealthy family in Dublin, Ireland, in 1889. During his youth, he was hit in the ear by a cricket ball; consequently, his hearing was impaired in that ear for the rest of his life. At the age of 24, he became aware of the extreme poverty of many people in the cities of Ireland and tried to make a difference by serving the poor in Dublin through the Society of St. Vincent de Paul. This charitable work gave him a desire to lead a more devout Christian life. As a result, he started to attend two Masses a day beginning in 1914, and continued this practice for the rest of his life.

With his dear friend Venerable Edel Quinn, Duff became a pioneer of lay involvement in apostolic works. He greatly encouraged the Catholic laity to strive for sanctity and engage in charitable works. He was so well respected for his contributions to the apostolate of the laity that Bl. Pope Paul VI invited him to attend the Second Vatican Council as a lay observer. During the final session of the Council, the entire assembly of bishops from around the world stood and gave Frank Duff a standing ovation in recognition of his tremendous work. In his zeal to help souls experience the freedom that the truths of Catholicism bring, he was miraculously able to help bring about the conversion of almost the entire red-light district in Dublin, especially the area associated with prostitution. He was very devoted to the Sacred Heart of Jesus. Frank Duff lived to be 91 years old, dying on a First Friday.

Marian Devotion

In 1917, the same year that Our Lady appeared in Fatima and St. Maximilian founded the Militia Immaculatae, Frank Duff read St. Louis de Montfort's *True Devotion to the Blessed Virgin*. He had overheard a few men discussing the book and became interested in acquiring a copy himself. When he found a first edition of the English translation in a bookstore, he purchased it. At first, he did not understand the book due to its depth and lofty Marian expressions, but, after reading it half a dozen times, he finally got it. This devotion set his soul aflame. He understood that Mary was not just another saint and member of the Church, but the greatest of all saints and the very heart of the mystery of

Christianity. From this point on, he began to teach everyone that if they did not understand Mary, they were incapable of understanding Christianity.

As a result of his fervent devotion to Our Lady, he founded the Legion of Mary on September 7, 1921. Having been greatly influenced himself by the writings of St. Louis de Montfort, Duff established that the Legion was to be very Montfortian in its Marian devotion and piety. The purpose and goal of the Legion was to assist Mary, the Mediatrix of All Grace, in the spiritual combat perpetually waged between the Church and the powers of darkness. He named his organization the Legion of Mary because he viewed it as an army of the Mother of God, championing the cause of her divine Son. Through this army's use of prayer and apostolic works, he wanted the Legion to help the Church bring all souls to Jesus through Mary. It would prove to be an extremely fruitful Marian apostolate during the 20th century, with members in almost every diocese in the world. Blessed Pope Paul VI described the Legion of Mary as the greatest movement to help souls since the establishment of the great mendicant religious orders in the 16th century! It was so effective at bringing about conversions to Christ and spread so quickly to every part of the globe that Mao Tse-tung, the Communist leader and father of the People's Republic of China, referred to the Legion of Mary as "Public Enemy Number One."

Champion of the Rosary

A devoted son of the Church, Frank Duff spent at least four hours a day in prayer. On most days, he would even sacrifice his lunch break to spend an hour in prayer. The rosary was always part of his daily prayer routine. He was very fond of recommending the daily rosary to everyone he met. He had a unique understanding of the rosary, saying it is the "prime devotion to the Holy Spirit." What he meant was that when a person prays the rosary, they are immediately overshadowed by the Holy Spirit, since Mary is the Spouse of the Holy Spirit and can never be separated from her spouse. This dimension of his thought is quite fascinating, since people rarely associate devotion to the Holy Spirit with the recitation of the rosary. In the mind of Frank Duff, the rosary opens up hearts to the workings of the Holy Spirit because in the rosary we celebrate and remember the principal interventions of the Holy Spirit in the drama and mysteries of salvation.

The largest Marian association in the world, the Legion of Mary is made up of small local groups called "Praesidiums." This terminology comes from the Roman technique of protecting a particular area by maintaining a fortified garrison or military line. A Legion of Mary Praesidium conducts apostolic works and meets weekly to pray. Frank Duff mandated that each Praesidium pray the rosary as part of their weekly prayer meeting. He also encouraged each member to join the Confraternity of the Rosary.

Frank Duff always stressed that the rosary is the core of the Legion of Mary's spirituality. As such, he desired that the rosary be prayed with dignity and respect. He did not want it prayed too quickly or in a chaotic fashion, but rather, with a meditative rhythm. He particularly emphasized that those praying the second half of the Hail Mary were not to start before the person praying the first half of the Hail Mary had said the Holy Name of Jesus. Duff considered the rosary to be so essential to the Legion of Mary that, when he wrote the Legion of Mary handbook, he said that what breathing is to the human body, the rosary is to the Legion of Mary.

Rosary Gems

The rosary was established about the year 1200 and it took from the first minute. It was proposed to people and they were encouraged to use it. It proved itself to have an affinity for the people. Ever since, it has been intertwined with Catholic life. It has been prominent in devotional literature; an element in the lives of the holy ones of the Church; the subject of the teachings of the Popes and the Doctors. The rosary has been carried by Our Lady in many of the accepted apparitions. It has entered into many of the recorded miraculous events, some of which have saved the world. It is believed to have been responsible for innumerable favors. I wonder has there been any saint since the 13th century who did not use it?

~ Servant of God Frank Duff

Anyone who says the rosary will have a reasonably complete and vivid idea of the Christian narrative.

~ Servant of God Frank Duff

If the rosary be hurt [neglected], Mary's place will be diminished and so will the quantity of prayer in our lives.

~ Servant of God Frank Duff

The rosary is a prayer which fits itself to changing circumstances. At times of sickness or of exhaustion, there is no other so useful.

~ Servant of God Frank Duff

As we say the rosary, we try to stage the mysteries before our minds. However meager our powers to meditate, we cannot help learning all those mysteries. They expand into so many "photographic" situations, linking themselves up with the various pictures we have seen or the accounts which we have heard or read of those events. We may be sure too that grace takes hold of that "picturisation," intensifies it and renders it fruitful.

~ Servant of God Frank Duff

Every word of the rosary is a prayer to God.

~ Servant of God Frank Duff

The rosary counteracts any tendency to relegate her [Mary] to a sub-compartment in the Christian life.

~ Servant of God Frank Duff

The rosary should be recited reverently.

~ Servant of God Frank Duff

The rosary is irreplaceable.

~ Servant of God Frank Duff

POPE PIUS XI

The Watchman of the Rosary
1857–1939

PAPACY: 1922–1939

Pope Pius XI held the chair of St. Peter during the period between World War I and World War II. A man of blunt speech and a no-nonsense style of leadership, he took the name "Pius" because of the great admiration he had for the pope of his youth, Bl. Pope Pius IX. Pius XI was a very accomplished scholar and, before becoming pope, had served as the chief librarian for the Ambrosian Library in Milan; the Archbishop of Milan; and the prefect of the Vatican Library in Rome. He earned three doctorate degrees (in philosophy, theology, and canon law) from the Gregorian University in Rome and specialized in paleography (or the study of ancient handwriting), focusing on medieval manuscripts and documents. At one point, he also served as the apostolic nuncio to Poland and had such a tremendous zeal for Christian unity that he desired to be a martyr in Russia.

During his papacy, he canonized St. Bernadette Soubirous, St. John Vianney, St. Don Bosco, and St. Thérèse of Lisieux. He also established the Feast of Christ the King as a means of trying to ease tensions between various nations. He established Vatican Radio in 1931 and was the first pope to broadcast on radio. Like his predecessors, he strongly condemned Modernism and promoted unity and peace. An avid mountain climber, he reached the summit of many famous peaks, including the Matterhorn. There is even a glacier named after him in Chile.

Marian Devotion

Before he became pope, Pius XI was a member of a Jesuit sodality of Our Lady and was known to be a very Marian priest. When he became the archbishop of Milan, he started a Marian sodality in his archdiocese. He so loved the Sodality of Our Lady that he compared it to the Milky Way, stretching from horizon to horizon and encompassing countless souls. It was during his pontificate and with his knowledge and consent that the Fatima apparitions received approval by the Church. He called Lithuania the *Terra Mariana* ("the land of Mary") and, in 1930, declared the Immaculate Conception (under the title of "Our Lady of Aparecida") the Patroness of Brazil. He also greatly loved Lourdes and, one year before he was elected pope, made an official pilgrimage to Lourdes. Once pope, he canonized St. Bernadette Soubirous on December 8, 1933.

Providentially, it was one year before Pius XI was elected to the papacy that the Servant of God Frank Duff founded the Legion of Mary. During Pius XI's papacy, the Legion of Mary spread throughout the world, and on September 16, 1933, Pope Pius XI imparted a special blessing to all the members of the Legion of Mary. As part of this blessing, he noted that, just as Mary had cooperated in redemption, the members of the Legion of Mary were to be cooperators with Christ in his salvific mission. Pope Pius XI clearly taught that Mary rightly deserves the titles Mediatrix of All Grace and Co-Redemptrix.

Champion of the Rosary

During his pontificate, Pius XI dealt with the aftermath of World War I, the possibility of another world war, and the anti-Catholic persecutions in Mexico, Spain, and the Soviet Union. He warned the world of the errors of Fascism, Communism, and Nazism, and urged the recitation of the most holy rosary. To this purpose, in 1937, he wrote the rosary encyclical *Ingravescentibus Malis (The Ever-Worsening Evils)*. In this powerful encyclical, he affirmed that St. Dominic was the founder of the rosary, underscored that the rosary is a weapon to be used against all heresies, ideologies, and threats against truth, and made an appeal to all people to pray it. He taught that the rosary is a weapon for combating the evil spirits at work in the world and bringing about peace in the hearts of men. During his pontificate, many of the faithful who became martyrs gave witness to the rosary: Blessed Miroslav Bulešic, Blessed Ceferino Giménez Malla, Blessed Miguel Pro, and many others. Pius XI knew that the rosary had the power to conquer all ideologies, especially that of Communism.

A champion of the rosary, Pope Pius XI issued a decree ordering that the Basilica of Our Lady of the Rosary of Pompeii be expanded and enlarged so that more people could go there on pilgrimage. He emphasized that the rosary was not a vainly repetitious prayer, but rather could be compared to a person saying to their beloved "I love you" over and over again. He wrote a personal letter to the Master General of the Dominicans affirming the pious tradition, explicitly stating that Prouille was the cradle of the rosary, and told the Dominicans that the rosary is at the center of their charism and should be zealously promoted by the friars. He saw the rosary as a teacher of the moral and theological virtues, capable of cultivating in souls a desire for holiness and a greater love for Christ and the Church.

Rosary Gems

Among the weapons St. Dominic used to convert the heretics the most efficacious, as the faithful well know, was the Marian rosary, the practice of which, taught by the Blessed Virgin herself, has so widely spread throughout the Catholic world. Now where does the efficacy and power of this manner of praying come from? Certainly from the very mysteries of the Divine Redeemer which we contemplate and piously meditate so that we may rightly say that the Marian rosary contains the root and foundation on which the Order of St. Dominic depends, in order to procure the perfection of life of its own members and the salvation of other men.

~ Pope Pius XI

Saint Dominic founded the Order of Friars Preachers which Pope Honorius III placed under his own special protection and patronage and whose members he acclaimed, as it were, prophetically, "true lights of the world," and "champions of the faith." The first monastery was founded at Saint Mary of Prouille, which was, indeed, the cradle of the rosary of Mary itself.

~ Pope Pius XI

When very frequently we receive newly married couples in audience and address paternal words to them, we give them rosaries, we recommend these to them earnestly, and we exhort them, citing our own example, not to let even one day pass without saying the rosary, no matter how burdened they may be with many cares and labors.

~ Pope Pius XI

How could love not be made more fervent by the rosary? We meditate on the suffering and death of our Redeemer and the sorrows of his afflicted Mother.

~ Pope Pius XI

Kings and princes, burdened with most urgent occupations and affairs, made it their duty to recite the rosary.

~ Pope Pius XI

Among the various supplications with which we successfully appeal to the Virgin Mother of God, the holy rosary without doubt occupies a special and distinct place.

~ Pope Pius XI

The rosary enlivens the hope for things above that endure forever. As we meditate on the glory of Jesus and his Mother, we see heaven opened and are heartened in our striving to gain the eternal home.

~ Pope Pius XI

The fathers and mothers of families particularly must give an example to their children, especially when, at sunset, they gather together after the day's work, within the domestic walls, and recite the holy rosary on bended knees before the image of the Virgin, together fusing voice, faith and sentiment. This is a beautiful and salutary custom, from which certainly there cannot but be derived tranquility and abundance of heavenly gifts for the household.

~ Pope Pius XI

Those wander from the path of truth who consider this devotion [the rosary] merely an annoying formula repeated with monotonous singsong intonation, and refuse it as good only for children and silly women!

~ Pope Pius XI

This mystic crown [the rosary], not only is found in and glides through the hands of the poor, but it also is honored by citizens of every social rank.

~ Pope Pius XI

Everyone can understand how salutary it [the rosary] is, especially in our times wherein sometimes a certain annoyance of the things of the spirit is felt even among the Faithful, and a dislike, as it were, for the Christian doctrine.

~ Pope Pius XI

The holy rosary not only serves admirably to overcome the enemies of God and Religion, but is also a stimulus and spur to the practice of evangelic virtues which it injects and cultivates in our souls. Above all, it nourishes the Catholic Faith, which flourishes again by due meditation on the sacred mysteries, and raises minds to the truth revealed to us by God.

~ Pope Pius XI

The rosary elevates minds to the truths revealed by God and shows us Heaven opened. The Virgin Mary herself has insistently recommended this manner of praying. All graces are conceded to us by God through the hands of Mary.

~ Pope Pius XI

BLESSED JAMES ALBERIONE
The Evangelist of the Rosary
1884–1971

BEATIFIED: April 27, 2003 by St. John Paul II
FEAST DAY: November 26

BLESSED JAMES ALBERIONE was born in northern Italy and was one of the greatest pioneers in the field of Catholic media. When asked by his first grade teacher what he wanted to be when he grew up, he said that he wanted to be a priest. An erudite theologian, he earned a doctorate in theology and served for a time as a seminary professor and spiritual director. In his zeal to use modern means of social communication to spread the Gospel, he founded the Pauline family, consisting of 10 religious institutes for priests, religious, and laity.

He was ahead of his time in his ardor for using social communication as a means of spreading the Gospel. His work was so well respected that he was invited to attend every session of the Second Vatican Council as a theological consultant. Blessed Pope Paul VI greatly admired and supported his work, and took the time to visit Bl. James on his deathbed; an hour after the papal visit, Bl. James died. He was buried in the basilica he had had constructed in Rome, the Basilica of Mary, Queen of Apostles. Saint John Paul II referred to him as the first apostle of the New Evangelization and beatified him on Divine Mercy Sunday in 2003.

Marian Devotion

From his earliest days, Bl. James manifested a profound devotion to Mary. Shortly after his birth, his mother consecrated him to Our Lady at the Shrine of Our Lady of the Flowers in northern Italy. All throughout his youth, he frequented this Marian shrine and spent countless hours in prayer to Mary. As a priest, he desired that everything be done under the watchful and maternal gaze of Mary. Some of his greatest Marian influences were Blessed William Joseph Chaminade, St. Vincent Pallotti, and Pope Leo XIII. Blessed Alberione's Marian devotion led to personal sanctification and zealous apostolic activity. For this reason, in addition to stressing the importance of Mary's motherhood for each Christian, he also emphasized Mary's important apostolic work as our teacher and Co-Redemptrix. One of his favorite titles for Our Lady was "Queen of the Apostles."

Blessed Alberione wrote many prayers to Our Lady and also composed a chaplet to Mary, Queen of Apostles. He so loved Mary's title "Queen of the Apostles" that he saw to the construction of a new basilica in Rome to honor her under that same title. Mary was his favorite and most frequent topic when he preached. His writings on Our Lady total over 1,700 pages! He never missed an opportunity to introduce Mary into his many activities and apostolic works.

Champion of the Rosary

Blessed James Alberione often remarked that if Our Lady were to become more known, imitated, invoked, and loved, the world would be completely "Christianized." He particularly stressed that the Christianization of the world would come about through the weapon of the rosary. Like so many before him, he believed in the pious tradition about the rosary's origins and frequently referenced the many battles that had been won for Christ and the Church through the power of the rosary. Whether he was teaching, preaching, or authoring books, he always provided numerous examples of the power of the rosary in the lives of the saints. He loved to refer to the heroic example of the saints who found in the rosary a great source of sanctity, strength, protection, and zeal in their apostolic actions.

Whenever Bl. Alberione was about to give a talk, it was his practice to pray a rosary before delivering the talk. When traveling by car, he would pray non-stop rosaries until he reached his destination. He held that the rosary is an easy and efficacious prayer, especially helpful for growing in virtue and overcoming the enemies of the spiritual life. Knowing the rosary to be a prayer most pleasing to Our Lady, he emphasized praying the rosary with faith, devotion, and a firm purpose of reforming one's life. For this reason, he strongly encouraged people to pray the rosary on their knees when possible. He himself gave this pious example.

Rosary Gems

What is the rosary? It is the object of our hope. Afflicted sons and daughters, as soon as they hold the rosary in their hands, feel a new hope arising again in them, a hope which is strong and serene. After the cross I do not know of anything which can give comfort to a soul more than the rosary. The Church recommends the rosary to everyone, and desires that religious have it always with them so that they may live under the continual protection of Mary.

~ Blessed James Alberione

In the early times of the Church, the faithful made use of a kind of rosary consisting of a thin cord with many knots to count the prayers which they repeated. St. Dominic, inspired by God, gave a definite form to the rosary beads. This is a common belief and is also confirmed by many pontifical documents.

~ Blessed James Alberione

The Albigensians, a revolutionary and sacrilegious group, were denying truths of the Faith and devastating beautiful regions in France, Spain and Italy. At first St. Dominic tried to oppose them with his apostolic words, but to no avail. He then had recourse to Mary. He recited the holy rosary and had all the people recite it, too, while meditating on the mysteries. Mary won, and peace returned.

~ Blessed James Alberione

St. Dominic is the apostle of truth, but he is also the devout apostle of devotion to the rosary.

~ Blessed James Alberione

The Albigensians were conquered and converted in large numbers by St. Dominic with the holy rosary.

~ Blessed James Alberione

From her [Mary], St. Thomas Aquinas sought celestial wisdom daily with the holy rosary.

~ Blessed James Alberione

The rosary has obtained great conversions such as those of Ratisbonne and Hermann Cohen; it has given strength in battles against violent temptations, as experienced by St. Alphonsus and St. Francis de Sales; it has preserved baptismal innocence, as in St. Louis Gonzaga and in St. Rose of Lima.

~ Blessed James Alberione

St. Philip Neri walked the streets of Rome with the rosary in his hand; he sought out wayward souls and by means of the rosary inspired them to repent.

~ Blessed James Alberione

Whenever St. Vincent Pallotti, apostle of Rome, went to visit the dying, he would recite the rosary on the way.

~ Blessed James Alberione

St. Clement Hofbauer, apostle of Vienna, attributed to Mary the great conversions he obtained among sinners and the dying. Before dealing with them, he would recite and have others recite a part of the rosary.

~ Blessed James Alberione

St. Francis de Sales was a most meek and most strong priest; a bishop of inexhaustible zeal, a writer and preacher of true devotion; a marvel because of his prodigies. Why? He overcame the hardest trials by making a vow to recite the entire rosary daily, and he kept his vow faithfully.

~ Blessed James Alberione

St. John Berchmans died clutching the crucifix, the rosary, and the rules of his order. "These were the three things dearest to me during my life," he kept saying, "with these I die happily."

~ Blessed James Alberione

St. Louis IX, King of France, recited the rosary even while leading his army in time of war.

~ Blessed James Alberione

He [St. Charles Borromeo] instituted the Confraternity of the Rosary [in his diocese] and ordained that a solemn procession in honor of Mary, during which the Litany of the Blessed Virgin Mary was sung, be held in every parish on the first Saturday of every month. One night he was saying his evening prayers and the holy rosary, when a scoundrel broke into his quarters and fired a shot at him from close range. At the sound of the shot, the prayer ceased. Astonishment and terror seized those present, and although apparently mortally wounded, the saint smiled and calmly indicated to proceed with the prayers. At their conclusion, St. Charles Borromeo rose, and to his great surprise saw the bullet, which had barely ripped his outer garment, fall at his feet.

~ Blessed James Alberione

The rosary is an easy, powerful, and common devotion.

~ Blessed James Alberione

How often a rosary, a medal of the Blessed Mother, devout novenas, penances for the salvation of obstinate sinners who are ill, have obtained real prodigies from this Mother!

~ Blessed James Alberione

Let us recite the holy rosary often and well.

~ Blessed James Alberione

Toward Mary we must have an enlightened and limitless confidence and love; the most heartfelt, expansive, and tender devotion; the most common and constant practices of the rosary, the Angelus, the three Hail Marys, the chaplet, Saturday, etc.

~ Blessed James Alberione

The rosary is a compendium of the Holy Gospel; it is a summary of the lives of Our Lord and the Virgin Mary; it is a summary of the entirety of Christian doctrine. Therefore, it has justly been called the Christian's Breviary.

~ Blessed James Alberione

The rosary is an easy devotion. It is composed of prayers which everyone learns as a child — prayers which can be said without any effort or difficulty. The rosary can be recited at any time, in any place and in any circumstance. The rosary is pleasing to the Blessed Virgin, because of its origin and its excellence. In fact, the rosary is not the product of human fancy; it was suggested to men by the Blessed Virgin herself, and she had the most sublime purpose for doing so. Mary personally gave us this precious token of salvation, and she also taught us the manner of using it. Is there any devotion [to Mary] more excellent than this?

~ Blessed James Alberione

More than once, through the rosary, those who were disseminating grave errors have been defeated. Through it many sinners have been converted to God; through it love of God and of his mother has bloomed anew. The Church herself has found in the rosary her shield of defense. With this mighty weapon she has defeated Satan, just as with a sling David defeated the giant Goliath. It is not without reason that the Supreme Pontiffs have strongly recommended this practice, enriching it with indulgences.

~ Blessed James Alberione

As long as the rosary remains in a family, Jesus, [the] Way and Truth and Life, remains.

~ Blessed James Alberione

Mary's merits for our redemption shine forth in the mysteries of the rosary.

~ Blessed James Alberione

Without the rosary, I felt I was incapable of even giving an exhortation.

~ Blessed James Alberione

Let us resolve to pray to the Blessed Virgin especially with the recitation of the rosary.

~ Blessed James Alberione

Always, everything was built more with the rosary than with other means.

~ Blessed James Alberione

Queen of the Most Holy Rosary, in these times of such brazen impiety, manifest thy power with the signs of thine ancient victories.

~ Blessed James Alberione

Jesus cried over Jerusalem, which did not want to listen to him. He cried seeing the punishment that would touch this city. And when you are not received, feel sad, not for yourselves, but for them, and recite the rosary for them.

~ Blessed James Alberione

Say many and beautiful rosaries. We show our devotion to Mary, Queen of Apostles, especially through the simple form of the rosary.

~ Blessed James Alberione

The rosary, which the Church so highly recommends, is not only the font of many graces for the living, but also a most powerful means of aiding the dead.

~ Blessed James Alberione

The rosary is a prayer for the evangelization of the pagans, for the conversion of heretics, for the return of schismatics, for making lukewarm and superficial Christians fervent; for leading good Christians to sanctity.

~ Blessed James Alberione

The rosary of Mary is the great lever, it is the anchor of salvation for society and for individuals. Lepanto and Vienna are names associated with the rosary. The victories over the Albigensians, over French philosophism, over liberalism and modernism find their explanation in the rosary.

~ Blessed James Alberione

Following one's vocation means waging a continuous battle because the devil will make every effort to ruin vocations. Thus, the rosary is the great means of victory.

~ Blessed James Alberione

The rosary can be recited everywhere: on the street, in the train, in the bus, in church, in waiting rooms — all places can be considered suitable for reciting the rosary.

~ Blessed James Alberione

Recite the rosary with the humility of [St.] Bernadette or of the three little shepherds of Fatima.

~ Blessed James Alberione

VENERABLE POPE PIUS XII

The Pastor of the Rosary
1876–1958

PAPACY: 1939–1958
VENERABLE: December 19, 2009 by Pope Benedict XVI

VENERABLE POPE PIUS XII was born in Rome in 1876 to a devout family who instilled in his heart a deep desire for prayer. His father was a particularly pious Third Order Franciscan and helped his young son discern a call to the priesthood. Ordained on Easter Sunday, he served in a variety of capacities as a priest. Pope Benedict XV consecrated him a bishop in the Sistine Chapel on the same day that Mary was making her first appearance in Fatima (May 13, 1917). Years later, after having served the Church as the papal nuncio to Germany, he was elected to the chair of St. Peter and took the name "Pius" because of his great respect for Pope Pius XI.

Always a critic of Nazism, Pius XII helped many Jewish people escape from Poland during WWII, and even hid many Jews in the Vatican. These actions so impressed the chief rabbi of Rome, Rabbi Israel Zolli, that in 1945, after the war, he converted to Catholicism. Pius XII is responsible for making Karol Wojtyła (the future St. John Paul II) a bishop at the young age of 38. Pius XII wrote 41 encyclicals and canonized a number of great Marian saints, including St. Louis de Montfort, St. Catherine Labouré, and St. Anthony Mary Claret. After the Sacred Scriptures, he is the most frequently cited authoritative source in the documents from the Second Vatican Council. Venerable Pope Pius XII died on October 9, 1958, and was buried at St. Peter's on October 13, the anniversary of the Miracle of the Sun at Fatima.

Marian Devotion

Venerable Pope Pius XII is often called the "Pope of Mary" because of his tender love for the Virgin. When he was a young boy, he would spend hours in prayer before an image of Mary at the Gesu, the Jesuit church and general headquarters in Rome. This pious practice often made him late for dinner. When he was ordained a priest, he requested that his first Mass be celebrated before the altar of the *Salus Populi Romani* image of Mary in the Basilica of Santa Maria Maggiore. Upon becoming pope, he explicitly placed his pontificate under the care of Our Lady of Good Counsel and encouraged all priests to have a tender devotion toward her.

He is also known as the "Pope of the Assumption" because, in 1950, he officially declared the dogma that Mary was assumed, body and soul, into heaven. According to Sr. M. Pascalina Lehnert, his housekeeper for 40 years, Pius XII saw the "miracle of the sun" — similar to that which occurred at Fatima — on four separate occasions. Three of these occurrences were within days of the proclamation of the dogma of the Assumption, and one of them occurred on November 1, 1950, the actual day of the definition.

Pius XII's writings are rich in Marian theology and devotion. In 1947, addressing the Marian Congress in Ottawa, Canada, he noted that because Mary is the mother of the Vine (Jesus), she is also the mother of the branches (us). During the Marian Year 1953–1954, which he himself declared, he personally crowned the image of the *Salus Populi Romani* and wrote a beautiful prayer, calling her the "Conqueress of evil and death." In *Mystici Corporis,* his theologically profound encyclical on the Church, he described Mary as the neck and heart of the Mystical Body through which all graces flow. He celebrated the centenary of the proclamation of the dogma of the Immaculate Conception in his letter *Fulgens Corona,* and in *Mediator Dei,* his encyclical on the liturgy, he emphasized that the month of May was to be particularly dedicated to Mary. Additionally, he wrote an encyclical commemorating the centenary of Lourdes, established the Feast of the Queenship of Mary, and wrote the document considered the "magna carta" for the Sodality of Mary, titled *Bis Saeculari.* He so greatly loved the Marian Sodality that he is also known as the "Pope of the Sodalities." He personally erected the World Federation of Sodalities and spoke at the First International Sodality World Congress on September 8, 1954.

Champion of the Rosary

As a devoted son of Mary, it was only natural for Pius XII to also have a deep love for the rosary. In 1942, on the 25th anniversary of the apparitions at Fatima, with World War II raging, he explicitly invoked the intercession of the Queen of the Most Holy Rosary, asking her to bring about peace in the world. Like so many others before him, he understood the rosary to be a weapon and, in particular, stressed that the rosary is similar to

David's sling: small, but able to bring down the mighty Goliath. He emphasized that the rosary has pride of place among all the devotions to Mary. When he consecrated the world to the Immaculate Heart of Mary in 1942, he explicitly mentioned the Marian title "Queen of the Rosary." In 1946, he wrote a letter to the archbishop of Manila called *Philippinas Insulas*, and referred to the rosary as the *"totius Evangelii breviarum"* ("a summary of the entire Gospel"). During the Marian Congress in the Philippines in 1954, Pius XII delivered a message to it by radio, stating that the rosary is the national devotion of the country and calling the Philippines the "Kingdom of the Holy Rosary." In his audiences with newlyweds, he always exhorted them to pray the rosary throughout their marriage and encouraged parents to teach their children to lay the spiritual flowers of the rosary at the feet of Mary's images.

In 1952, he published the profound rosary encyclical *Ingruentium Malorum (The Approaching Evils)*, stressing that the origins of the rosary are heavenly rather than human. In this deeply beautiful encyclical, he also attaches particular importance to the promotion of the family rosary as a means of preserving the faith in children and helping adults acquire virtue and perseverance in their Christian journey. During his papacy, he prayed the rosary at various times throughout his busy day, and constantly encouraged priests to pray the daily rosary as a means of growing in holiness. In 1957, he wrote a personal letter to the Master General of the Dominicans to remind the sons of St. Dominic that the promotion of the rosary is a particular mark of the Dominican order, and that they were to continue to zealously, diligently, and devoutly promote it.

Rosary Gems

There is no surer means of calling down God's blessings upon the family and especially of preserving peace and happiness in the home than the daily recitation of the rosary. And apart from its supplicatory power, the family rosary can have very far-reaching effects, for if the habit of this pious practice is inculcated into children at a young and impressionable age, they too will be faithful to the rosary in later years, and their faith will thereby be nourished and strengthened.

~ Venerable Pope Pius XII

The Marian rosary is a marvelous garland woven from the angelic annunciation interspersed with the Lord's Prayer and joined together with a course of meditation, a most efficacious kind of entreaty, and most especially fruitful for the attainment of everlasting life. For this reason, in addition to the most excellent prayers of which it is comprised and which are, as it were, plaited into a crown of heavenly roses, it also offers an invitation to stir up one's faith, a help to devotion and outstanding models of virtue through the mysteries presented for contemplation. It therefore cannot fail to be most pleasing to the Virgin Mother of God and to her only Son, who undoubtedly considers any praise, honor and glory rendered to his mother as likewise rendered to himself.

~ Venerable Pope Pius XII

If you recite the family rosary, all united, you shall taste peace; you shall have in your homes concord of souls.

~ Venerable Pope Pius XII

The flowers of the rosary never perish.

~ Venerable Pope Pius XII

We put great confidence in the holy rosary for the healing of evils which afflict our times. Not with force, not with arms, not with human power, but with Divine help obtained through the means of this prayer, strong like David with his sling, the Church undaunted shall be able to confront the infernal enemy.

~ Venerable Pope Pius XII

O sorrowful and Immaculate Heart of Mary, Queen of the Most Holy Rosary, and Queen of the World, rule over us, together with the Sacred Heart of Jesus Christ, our King. Save us from the spreading flood of modern paganism; kindle in our hearts and homes the love of purity, the practice of a virtuous life, an ardent zeal for souls, and a desire to pray the rosary more faithfully.

~ Venerable Pope Pius XII

There are certain exercises of piety which the Church recommends very much to clergy and religious. It is our wish also that the faithful, as well, should take part in these practices. The chief of these are: meditation on spiritual things, diligent examination of conscience, enclosed retreats, visits to the Blessed Sacrament, and those special prayers in honor of the Blessed Virgin Mary, among which the rosary, as all know, has pride of place.

~ Venerable Pope Pius XII

What a sweet sight — most pleasing to God — when, at eventide, the Christian home resounds with the frequent repetition of praises in honor of the august Queen of Heaven! Then the rosary, recited in common, assembles before the image of the Virgin, in an admirable union of hearts, the parents and their children, who come back from their daily work. It unites them piously with those absent and those dead. It links all more tightly in a sweet bond of love, with the most Holy Virgin, who, like a loving mother, in the circle of her children, will be there bestowing upon them an abundance of the gifts of concord and family peace.

~ Venerable Pope Pius XII

The home of the Christian family, like that of Nazareth, will become an earthly abode of sanctity, and, so to speak, a sacred temple, where the holy rosary will not only be the particular prayer which every day rises to heaven in an odor of sweetness, but will also form the most efficacious school of Christian discipline and Christian virtue. This meditation on the Divine Mysteries of the Redemption will teach the adults to live, admiring daily the shining examples of Jesus and Mary, and to draw from these examples comfort in adversity, striving towards those heavenly treasures "where neither thief draws near, nor moth destroys" (Luke 12:33). This meditation will bring to the knowledge of the little ones the main truths of the Christian Faith, making love for the Redeemer blossom almost spontaneously in their innocent hearts, while, seeing their parents kneeling before the majesty of God, they will learn from their very early years how great before the throne of God is the value of prayers said in common.

~ Venerable Pope Pius XII

We consider the holy rosary the most convenient and most fruitful means [to obtain the aid of Mary], as is clearly suggested by the very origin of this practice, heavenly rather than human, and by its nature. What prayers are better adapted and more beautiful than the Lord's prayer and the angelic salutation, which are the flowers with which this mystical crown is formed? With meditation on the Sacred Mysteries added to the vocal prayers, there emerges another very great advantage, so that all, even the most simple and least educated, have in this a prompt and easy way to nourish and preserve their own faith.

~ Venerable Pope Pius XII

Queen of the Most Holy Rosary, Help of Christians, Refuge of Mankind, triumphant in all battles for God! We, your suppliants, prostrate ourselves at your throne, confident that we shall obtain mercy and receive grace, the needed assistance and protection, during the calamities of these days, not indeed by our own merits, of which we presume nothing, but solely through the immense goodness of your maternal heart.

~ Venerable Pope Pius XII

Let all try to approach with greater trust the throne of grace and mercy of our Queen and Mother, and beg for strength in adversity, light in darkness, consolation in sorrow; above all let them strive to free themselves from the slavery of sin and offer an unceasing homage, filled with filial loyalty, to their Queenly Mother. Let her churches be thronged by the faithful, her feast-days honored; may the beads of the rosary be in the hands of all; may Christians gather, in small numbers and large, to sing her praises in churches, in homes, in hospitals, in prisons. May Mary's name be held in highest reverence, a name sweeter than honey and more precious than jewels; may none utter blasphemous words, the sign of a defiled soul, against that name graced with such dignity and revered for its motherly goodness; let no one be so bold as to speak a syllable which lacks the respect due to her name.

~ Venerable Pope Pius XII

This [the rosary] is truly the national devotion of the Philippines, which remains sometimes the last link with the faith and the union of Christians in certain small islands of the North, so far that they seem lost in the fog, so remote, that they haven't seen missionaries for years and years. Philippines! Kingdom of Mary! Philippines! Kingdom of the Holy Rosary! Run to this throne of grace, to this saving devotion, because the storm is raging not far away from you. Remain firm in the Holy Faith of your fathers that you have received at the cradle, just as your islands remain firm, although shaken by earthquakes and violently besieged by irritated waves. And never let the sacred fire of your love for your heavenly Mother die in your souls, this sacred fire represented by these volcanoes erupting from time to time revealing the furnace hidden in your land.

~ Venerable Pope Pius XII

SERVANT OF GOD DOLINDO RUOTOLO

The White Martyr of the Rosary
1882–1970

THE SERVANT OF GOD DOLINDO RUOTOLO was born in Naples and is almost unknown outside of Italy. His unique name, "Dolindo," means "pain," and indeed, he was a white-martyr throughout his life. Saint Pio of Pietrelcina considered him a saint. Frequently, when people went to San Giovanni Rotondo to visit Padre Pio, he would ask why they were visiting him when there was a saint in Naples! Like St. Pio, Dolindo Ruotolo was zealous for the faith and frequently misunderstood by both the hierarchy and contemporary theologians.

Ruotolo was a priest with a Neapolitan temperament, not known to mince words when it came to opposing the historical-critical method of scripture scholarship. He zealously wrote against its abuse and warned people of its dangers. As a result, he had his priestly faculties to publicly celebrate the Sacraments removed on several occasions. To this day, there is a story circulating in Naples that Our Lady appeared to Venerable Pope Pius XII and exhorted him to give priestly faculties back to Dolindo immediately. Providentially, Pius XII intervened so that Dolindo could once again publicly celebrate the Sacraments. A devout priest and avid scholar, Dolindo has been called the "Scribe of the Holy Spirit." He penned a 33-volume commentary on Holy Scripture, as well as many other theological works. He wanted people to read good books on theology and devotion, and so he founded the Apostolato Stampa press in order to publish orthodox theological works. He was an extraordinary musician, a Third Order Franciscan, and slept less than three hours a night due to his intense prayer life.

Marian Devotion

An erudite theologian and author, Dolindo wrote many works on Our Lady and various commentaries on the Magnificat and the Visitation of Mary to her relative Elizabeth. He understood Our Lady to be at the very heart of Christianity and theology, and included her in almost all of his theological writings. During the last 10 years of his life, he referred to himself as "the Madonna's little old man." In his old age, he suffered from extreme arthritis and paralysis, yet persevered through the pain to write a trilogy of books on Our Lady. His Marian trilogy was written to defend the Marian teachings of the Church.

Dolindo was very devoted to both Our Lady of Lourdes and the message of Fatima. He zealously promoted devotion to the Immaculate Heart of Mary and emphasized that May was Mary's month. The month of May was particularly prominent in his devotion to Mary because he understood the human heart to be like a flower that needs to be cultivated by Mary. He also had a special love for the souls in purgatory. In the course of his various devotions to Mary, he offered up all his actions to Mary in order to help the poor souls in purgatory.

Champion of the Rosary

Throughout his priesthood, it was rare for anyone to see the Servant of God Dolindo Ruotolo without a rosary in his hand. The rosary was his constant companion. An accomplished musician, he was very fond of referring to the rosary in musical terms and considered the rosary to be his "spiritual" instrument. He deeply regretted that Modernism had reduced the prominence of the rosary in the lives of many Catholics, and emphatically preached that the rosary was not a tedious prayer of repetition, but a method for contemplating the saving mysteries of the life of Christ. He always encouraged people to pray the rosary devoutly and stressed that a rosary well prayed is analogous to laying roses at Mary's feet. On the other hand, he was quick to note that a rosary poorly prayed is comparable to laying dead leaves at the feet of the Queen of Heaven.

Dolindo lived through both World War I and World War II. He saw the rosary as a weapon in the spiritual life, referring to the rosary as a sword and a machine gun in our spiritual arsenal. In his homilies, he often informed his listeners that every Hail Mary was a shot fired at Satan and the forces of darkness. He had a profound understanding of Our Lady's necessary role in bringing us closer to Christ, and believed Our Lady to be the Mediatrix of All Grace and the spiritual "power grid" that distributes all the graces of Christ to the members of the Church. Extending the metaphor, he emphasized that the rosary was a major means of tapping into the power grid.

Rosary Gems

In climbing toward God for its salvation, the soul possesses the Key of Heaven in the rosary.

~ Servant of God Dolindo Ruotolo

Amid the disharmony of our chaotic lives, the rosary is the instrument, the harp or the psaltery with its ten chords, for each group of harmonies. With the rosary we continually raise a song of love from earth.

~ Servant of God Dolindo Ruotolo

The rosary has very great riches, both in the Hail Mary and in the mysteries contemplated. It is not a monotonous mumbling. It is a marvelous harmony, just as a musical instrument does not play a dull repetition of a note, but a melodic and harmonious variation, which raises the soul and arouses in it much affection and sweet and pure thoughts. It is almost a vibration of waves and the delicacy of musical chords.

~ Servant of God Dolindo Ruotolo

As an army has its marching music, marking the time for the soldiers, so does the rosary lovingly mark time for the Church militant.

~ Servant of God Dolindo Ruotolo

The rosary is a powerful prayer against Satan and against the assaults of evil. Our Church brought, and continues to bring, great triumphs because of this prayer. The decades of the rosary, from this point of view, are like the belt of a machine gun: every bead is a shot, every affection of the soul is as an explosion of faith that frightens off Satan, and Mary once more crushes his head.

~ Servant of God Dolindo Ruotolo

O Most Holy Rosary, may your flowers bloom on the desolate flowerbeds of unbelievers and let simple and lively faith come to bloom again.

~ Servant of God Dolindo Ruotolo

The holy rosary was always, and still is the most acceptable devotion to the Heart of Mother Mary.

~ Servant of God Dolindo Ruotolo

The rosary is not a tedious prayer just because the person is always repeating the Hail Mary. Each Hail Mary recited, with the contemplation of the mysteries, is always said with a different feeling and the intensity of the prayer is not monotonous. It is an intensity of love. Does not a child call his mother all the time? His cry: "Mom!" is different according to the need that inspires and animates it. Therefore, recite the rosary like a child, invoking our Heavenly Mother and imploring her help.

~ Servant of God Dolindo Ruotolo

If you want to live a holy life, cultivate devotion to Mary in your family. Gather your children in prayer and in the recitation of the holy rosary.

~ Servant of God Dolindo Ruotolo

Praying the rosary is like the rolling of the pictures of a movie, a reminder of the great mysteries of our Redemption, showing them over and over again.

~ Servant of God Dolindo Ruotolo

The rosary saves you from despair and opens to you the luminous ways of charity and holiness. The rosary is your comfort in your life and the sweet chain that unites you to God.

~ Servant of God Dolindo Ruotolo

The rosary is not a tedious prayer in which we repeat always the same thing. This is the belief of those who look for an excuse not to say it.

~ Servant of God Dolindo Ruotolo

A careless rosary is a rosary with torn dead leaves.

~ Servant of God Dolindo Ruotolo

St. Pio of Pietrelcina

The Mystic
of the Rosary
1887–1968

BEATIFIED: May 2, 1999 by St. John Paul II
CANONIZED: June 16, 2002 by St. John Paul II
FEAST DAY: September 23

SAINT PIO OF PIETRELCINA, affectionately known as Padre Pio, was a Capuchin Franciscan and one of the greatest mystics of the 20th century. For more than 50 years, he bore the stigmata (bleeding wound marks) of Christ. He was a man of suffering and frequently misunderstood by his brother priests and religious confreres. Due to these misunderstandings, he was not allowed to hear confessions or celebrate Mass publicly for two years. Pope Pius XI, however, personally ordered the Holy Office to reverse the decisions made against Padre Pio.

Even while Padre Pio was alive, Venerable Pope Pius XII considered him a saint and encouraged people to visit the holy Franciscan mystic in San Giovanni Rotondo, the place where St. Pio lived and eventually opened a hospital. In 1947, Karol Józef Wojtyła, a young Polish priest studying in Rome, visited Padre Pio in San Giovanni Rotondo. Many people believe that during this encounter between the two future saints, the Franciscan mystic informed his Polish visitor of his future election to the papacy. Whether this is true or not, it was providentially planned that Wojtyła would be elected to the papacy, take the name John Paul II, and beatify and canonize St. Pio of Pietrelcina.

Marian Devotion

In line with the great Franciscan tradition of Marian spirituality, St. Pio understood Our Lady to be the tabernacle of the Most High, perpetually surrounded by angels. He was always aware that Mary was standing by his side as his mother and protector. A mystic who experienced frequent visions of Jesus, Mary, the saints, and the angels throughout his life, St. Pio was surprised when he learned that everyone else did not have similar visions. He would often ask his guardian angel to help him love Mary more, and frequently said that during the Mass, he felt the presence of Our Lady and the holy angels at his side.

A devoutly Marian priest, St. Pio offered fraternal guidance to his brother priests regarding Mary. He would inform them that they would only become holy and their ministries fruitful if they welcomed Mary into their hearts and maintained a deep relationship with her. His priestly heart was on fire with love for Mary; he knew that there is no other path leading to life except the one trod by our spiritual mother.

Mary obtained a healing for him on at least one occasion in 1959, when the Fatima Pilgrim Statue was touring through cities in Italy. When the statue came to San Giovanni Rotondo, he desperately wanted to see her, but was so ill that, after making three attempts to view the pilgrim statue, he was not able to lift himself out of bed. As the helicopter carrying the pilgrim statue took off, he poured out his sorrow to Mary, expressing his disappointment at not being able to see her miraculous statue. Then, all of a sudden, the pilot inexplicably turned the helicopter around and headed back toward the monastery where Padre Pio was in bed! The pilot later attested that he had no explanation for why he veered off course and returned to circle several times above the monastery. Padre Pio and heaven knew the reason. Mary desired to grant her son's wish, and as an additional blessing, at the moment that the helicopter was circling over his monastery, Padre Pio felt his body tremble. He experienced a complete healing. In thanksgiving for the healing, Padre Pio sent a crucifix to Fatima. Then, a few months later, a delegation from the Blue Army presented him with a hand-carved statue of Our Lady of Fatima. He placed it in the sacristy where he prepared for Mass each day. In 1968, he died whispering the name he honored a thousand times a day: "Maria."

Champion of the Rosary

Saint Pio, who clearly lived the life of a victim-soul (one who has been called by God to share in a special way in the sufferings of Jesus and make reparation for the sins of the world), has been referred to as the "Living Rosary" since, as a mystic who bore the wounds of Christ, he lived the mysteries of the rosary more directly than most and always had a rosary in his hand. As a youth, he learned his tremendous love for the rosary from the example provided by his family. Every evening, his family would gather together to pray it. A devout Catholic family, they would even fast in honor of Our Lady of Mt. Carmel. During his youth, as well as during his time as a soldier stationed in Naples, he made frequent visits to the Shrine of Our Lady of the Rosary of Pompeii.

One of the many sufferings imposed on St. Pio by the Church was that he was forbidden to write about his mystical experiences.

That is why there exist very few writings by him on the rosary and the other great loves of his holy life. Nevertheless, he bore constant witness to the rosary in his many conversations with people. When priests came to see him, he always recommended the rosary to them. It has been said that his silent sermon was always the rosary. He prayed it constantly throughout the day. Once, when asked by his religious superior how many rosaries he had prayed that day, St. Pio responded, "Thirty-four!" On another occasion, when asked by a Franciscan confrere what prayer was most pleasing to Mary, he quickly responded that it was the rosary because she herself had taught it to us and continued to stress its importance in her various apparitions.

Saint Pio understood the rosary to be a powerful spiritual weapon, able to overcome theological errors and false political regimes. On several occasions, he bilocated to the prison cell of another great champion of the rosary, József Cardinal Mindszenty. Imprisoned for his radical opposition to Communism, Mindszenty was a Hungarian prelate who frequently preached that the rosary was the secret weapon of the Catholic Church against Communism. Padre Pio knew this, too, and greatly desired to hand on the spiritual weapon of the rosary to his spiritual children. The day before he died, when asked to offer a final exhortation to those around him, his advice was to love Mary, make her known, and always pray the rosary. When he died, not only did he have the name of Mary on his lips, but he also had the rosary in his hand.

Rosary Gems

Love the Blessed Mother and make her loved. Always say the rosary.

~ St. Pio of Pietrelcina

The rosary is a weapon in our hands with which we can overcome the devil's attacks.

~ St. Pio of Pietrelcina

Our Lady has never refused me a grace through the recitation of the rosary.

~ St. Pio of Pietrelcina

Go get my weapon [the rosary].

~ St. Pio of Pietrelcina

Love the Madonna and pray the rosary, for her rosary is the weapon against the evils of the world today.

~ St. Pio of Pietrelcina

The rosary, that is my weapon.

~ St. Pio of Pietrelcina

Satan always tries to destroy this prayer [the rosary], but he will never succeed. It is the prayer of her who triumphs over everything and everyone.

~ St. Pio of Pietrelcina

The rosary is the weapon that wins all battles.

~ St. Pio of Pietrelcina

It would be impossible to name all the many saints who discovered in the rosary a genuine path to growth in holiness. We need but mention Saint Louis Marie Grignion de Montfort, the author of an excellent work on the rosary, and, closer to ourselves, Padre Pio of Pietrelcina, whom I recently had the joy of canonizing.

~ St. John Paul II

St. Josemaría Escrivá

The Pilgrim of the Rosary
1902–1975

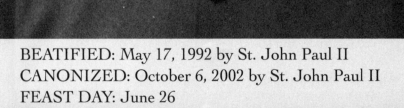

BEATIFIED: May 17, 1992 by St. John Paul II
CANONIZED: October 6, 2002 by St. John Paul II
FEAST DAY: June 26

SAINT JOSEMARÍA ESCRIVÁ was born in Barbastro, Spain, earned a doctorate in theology from the Lateran University in Rome, and lived his entire life in the 20th century. A very prayerful priest with a deep devotion to the Holy Eucharist, he worked with the poor and sick in the slums of Madrid for many years. In 1928, he founded Opus Dei, an organization of laypeople and priests dedicated to announcing God's universal call to holiness for all people. An extremely fruitful apostolate, Opus Dei received official approval from the Church in 1950 from Venerable Pope Pius XII.

Saint Josemaría Escrivá authored numerous books, many of which have been translated into multiple languages, selling millions of copies worldwide. Viktor Frankl, the famous psychiatrist, neurologist, and survivor of the Holocaust, once met St. Josemaría, and was so impressed and inspired by him that Frankl described him as a "spiritual atomic bomb."

Marian Devotion

At the age of two, St. Josemaría suffered from an unknown illness (most likely epilepsy) and was expected to die. His devout mother took him to the Marian shrine of Torreciudad in Aragon, Spain, and earnestly prayed for him before a statue of Our Lady of the Angels that dates from the 11th century. Miraculously, he recovered. His mother attributed his healing to Our Lady. This event helped to form in him a strong, life-long Marian devotion. As a seminarian, he made frequent visits to the nearby city of Saragossa to the Shrine of Our Lady of Pilar. Upon being ordained a priest, he celebrated his first Mass in that shrine. Later in life, always grateful for his healing as a child, he oversaw the construction of a major shrine to Our Lady in Torreciudad. This shrine continues to be operated by the members of Opus Dei and is a popular pilgrimage destination for people from all over Europe.

Throughout his life, St. Josemaría was known to have a particular love for Marian shrines and places where Mary had appeared in apparitions. He visited Fatima no less than nine times! On several of his trips to Fatima, he made personal visits to speak with the surviving visionary of Fatima, the Servant of God Sr. Lúcia Dos Santos. He loved to wander through the streets of

Rome in search of little images of Mary to honor and venerate, visited Lourdes several times, went on a pilgrimage to the shrine of Our Lady of the Rosary of Pompeii, and, in 1951, one year after Opus Dei received official approval, made a pilgrimage to the Holy House of Loreto to entrust Opus Dei completely to Our Lady. One of his favorite shrines was the one dedicated to Our Lady of Sonsoles in Spain. In Spanish, *sonsoles* means "those suns" and refers to the beautiful eyes of the Marian statue there. He made countless pilgrimages to lesser-known Marian shrines in Europe, as well, and in 1970, he traveled to Mexico City to make a novena at the Basilica of Our Lady of Guadalupe. Part of the heritage he left to the members of Opus Dei was his encouragement for the members to make frequent Marian pilgrimages.

Saint Josemaría never trusted any undertaking that didn't somehow manifest a love for Our Lady. He understood clearly that Jesus can only be truly found when we seek Mary, because it is God's will that we receive and return to Jesus through Mary. One of his greatest aspirations that he repeated constantly was the phrase, "*Omnes cum Petro ad Iesum per Mariam!*" ("All with Peter to Jesus through Mary!"). He ended almost all of his homilies by mentioning Mary, promoted devotion to the Brown Scapular, and taught that the month of May is a special time for Marian devotions. Every time he went into his room, he would kiss a particular statue of Our Lady; this statue became affectionately known as "The Lady of the Kisses." Once, after St. Josemaría venerated an image of St. Juan Diego giving a rose to Our Lady of Guadalupe, he expressed to those around him a desire to die in such fashion. Providentially, when he died in 1975, he was near a picture of Our Lady of Guadalupe that hung in his room.

Champion of the Rosary

Saint Josemaría's parents were devout Catholics. In his youth, they gave him the edifying example of praying the rosary in the home. At the age of 10, he began to carry the rosary in his pocket everywhere he went. He considered the rosary his weapon, his instructor in the virtues of Jesus and Mary, and a method for telling Mary that he loved her. A constant pilgrim, St. Josemaría always made the rosary a part of his Marian pilgrimages. He would pray the rosary during his journeys to shrines, as well as on the journeys back home. Even while at a shrine, he would make a point of walking around the grounds to pray a rosary.

Throughout his priestly life, he prayed the rosary every day and wrote a beautiful book on the rosary in just one day. In that book, he emphasized that the rosary should be prayed well, with a meditative spirit, and not in a hurried or rushed manner. He also emphasized that the rosary was not only for "little old women," but also for grown men and everyone else. Referencing the exhortation of Christ that only the childlike will enter the kingdom of heaven (see Mt 18:3), he instructed everyone that it is the rosary that most helps us to become childlike and express a daily love for the Blessed Virgin. To this day, the rosary remains a daily devotion at the shrine he founded in honor of Our Lady in Torreciudad, Spain. Part of his legacy to the members of Opus Dei was his example of praying the daily rosary, which he desired they imitate.

Rosary Gems

If you say the holy rosary every day, with a spirit of faith and love, Our Lady will make sure she leads you very far along her Son's path.

~ St. Josemaría Escrivá

Today, as in other times, the rosary must be a powerful weapon to enable us to win in our interior struggle, and to help all souls.

~ St. Josemaría Escrivá

The holy rosary is a powerful weapon. Use it with confidence and you'll be amazed at the results.

~ St. Josemaría Escrivá

To say the holy rosary, considering the mysteries, repeating the Our Father and Hail Mary, with the praises to the Blessed Trinity, and the constant invocation of the Mother of God, is a continuous act of faith, hope and love, of adoration and reparation.

~ St. Josemaría Escrivá

For a Christian, vocal prayer must spring from the heart, so that while the rosary is said, the mind can enter into contemplation of each one of the mysteries.

~ St. Josemaría Escrivá

You always leave the rosary for later, and you end up not saying it at all because you are sleepy. If there is no other time, say it in the street without letting anybody notice it. It will, moreover, help you to have presence of God.

~ St. Josemaría Escrivá

Many Christians have the custom of wearing the scapular; or they recall the central events in Christ's life by saying the rosary, never getting tired of repeating its words, just like people in love.

~ St. Josemaría Escrivá

When we say the rosary, which is a wonderful devotion which I will never tire of recommending to Christians everywhere, our minds and hearts go over the mysteries of Mary's admirable life which are, at the same time, the fundamental mysteries of our faith.

~ St. Josemaría Escrivá

Do you want to love Our Lady? Well, then, get to know her. How? By praying her rosary.

~ St. Josemaría Escrivá

Pray the holy rosary. Blessed be that monotony of Hail Marys which purifies the monotony of your sins!

~ St. Josemaría Escrivá

Pronounce the Our Father and the Hail Marys of each decade [of the rosary] clearly and without rushing: this will help you always to get more and more out of this way of loving Mary.

~ St. Josemaría Escrivá

Take [up] the rosary, one of the most deeply rooted of Christian devotions. The Church encourages us to contemplate its mysteries.

~ St. Josemaría Escrivá

Pause for a few seconds — three or four — in silent meditation to consider each mystery of the rosary before you recite the Our Father and the Hail Marys of that decade. I am sure this practice will increase your recollection and the fruits of your prayer.

~ St. Josemaría Escrivá

St. Pope John XXIII

The Shepherd of the Rosary
1881–1963

PAPACY: 1958–1963
BEATIFICATION: September 3, 2000 by St. John Paul II
CANONIZATION: April 27, 2014 by Pope Francis with
Pope Emeritus Benedict XVI in attendance
FEAST DAY: October 11

SAINT POPE JOHN XXIII was born in the Lombardy region of Italy and had 13 brothers and sisters. While in the seminary, he became a Third Order Franciscan. Over the course of his priestly life, he served the Holy See in several diplomatic assignments, including an appointment as the papal nuncio to France. During World War II, while nuncio, he helped save many Jewish people from the horrors of the Holocaust. Elected to the papacy in 1958, he was chosen to lead the Church during the initial years of the turbulent 1960s. Aware that there was a cultural shift occurring in society, he opened the historic Second Vatican Council in October of 1962. His frequent habit of sneaking out of the Vatican at night to walk the streets of Rome earned him the nickname "Johnny Walker." He is often referred to as the "Pope of St. Joseph" because he did much to promote devotion to St. Joseph.

He had a great sense of humor. Once, when asked how many people worked at the Vatican, he responded, "About half!" Good Pope John XXIII died of stomach cancer in 1963.

Marian Devotion

From his youth, John XXIII had a great love for Our Lady, especially Our Lady of Perpetual Help. As a priest, he showed a particular love for Marian shrines and visited them frequently. He visited Fatima in Portugal, Czestochowa in Poland, and Lourdes (his favorite Marian shrine) in France. He first went to Lourdes in 1905, and afterwards made numerous pilgrimages there as nuncio. During his time as archbishop of Venice, he consecrated the new Basilica of Lourdes on behalf of the pope.

He believed that piety towards the most holy Virgin was the mark of a truly Catholic heart. He did much to promote devotion to Mary during his pontificate. Prior to the opening of the Second Vatican Council, he journeyed to the Holy House of Loreto to ask for Mary's intercession for the Council. He is responsible for the canonization of many Marian saints, especially St. Vincent Pallotti and St. Peter Julian Eymard.

Champion of the Rosary

As a young child, St. Pope John XXIII loved the rosary and prayed it every evening with his family. He carried this love of the rosary into his priesthood; when he served as archbishop of Venice, he prayed 15 decades of the rosary every day. After he was elected to the papacy, the first encyclical of his pontificate was an encyclical on the rosary titled *Grata Recordatio* (*Grateful memory*). In it, he explicitly referred to and praised the rosary encyclicals of Pope Leo XIII, affirming that the rosary is a social remedy for the troubled times in which he was chosen to lead the Church.

His love of the rosary was so great that he established a daily schedule during his papacy that allowed him to pray the entire rosary every day. He would pray the Joyful Mysteries in the morning, the Sorrowful Mysteries in the afternoon, and, at 7:30 p.m. every evening, he would pray the Glorious Mysteries with the members of the papal household (his secretary, the religious sisters, and the housekeepers). He published a series of meditations on the various mysteries of the rosary, and noted that, after Holy Mass and the Liturgy of the Hours, the rosary has pride of place among all Christian devotions. He greatly supported the Servant of God Patrick Peyton in his efforts to promote rosary crusades and the family rosary, and encouraged everyone to pray the rosary. He considered the rosary to be the simplest and easiest form of prayer.

Rosary Gems

This prayer — the holy rosary — is the simplest and easiest one of all for the Christian people.

~ St. Pope John XXIII

When parents and children gather together at the end of the day in the recitation of the rosary, together they meditate on the example of work, obedience, and charity which shone in the house of Nazareth; together they learn from the Mother of God to suffer serenely; to accept with dignity and courage the difficulties of life and to acquire the proper attitude to the daily events of life. It is certain that they will meet with greater facility the problems of family life. Homes will thereby be converted into sanctuaries of peace. Torrents of divine favors will come to them, even the inestimable favor of a priestly or religious vocation.

~ St. Pope John XXIII

Individuals, whatever their spiritual status may be, will undoubtedly find in the fervent recitation of the holy rosary, an invitation to regulate their lives in conformity with Christian principles. They will, in truth, find in the rosary a spring of most abundant graces to help them in fulfilling faithfully their duties in life.

~ St. Pope John XXIII

The well-meditated rosary consists in a threefold element. For each decade there is a picture, and for each picture a threefold emphasis, which is simultaneously: mystical contemplation, intimate reflection, and pious intention.

~ St. Pope John XXIII

The rosary is a very commendable form of prayer and meditation. In saying it we weave a mystic garland of Ave Marias, Pater Nosters, *and* Gloria Patris.

~ St. Pope John XXIII

As an exercise of Christian devotion among the faithful of the Latin Rite who constitute a notable portion of the Catholic family, the rosary ranks after Holy Mass and the Breviary for ecclesiastics [priests], and for the laity after participation in the sacraments. It is a devout form of union with God and lifts souls to a high supernatural plane.

~ St. Pope John XXIII

May the rosary never fall from your hands.

~ St. Pope John XXIII

The rosary is the glory of the Roman Church.

~ St. Pope John XXIII

Oh, what a delight this blessed rosary is! Oh, what assurance it brings of being heard here on earth and in the eternal heavens!

~ St. Pope John XXIII

I knew Pope John. His love for Our Lady and his devotion to her rosary contributed an essential element to his spiritual growth and stature.

~ Servant of God Patrick Peyton

SERVANT OF GOD PATRICK PEYTON

The Rosary Priest
1909–1992

T HE SERVANT OF GOD PATRICK PEYTON was born into a poor family in Ireland. At the age of 19, he immigrated to the United States to find employment. He found work as a janitor at the Catholic cathedral in Scranton, Pennsylvania. On one occasion, he was so inspired by a mission preached by the Holy Cross Fathers that he joined their religious community and became a seminarian. While a seminarian, he was healed from tuberculosis as a result of praying a novena to Our Lady. In thanksgiving, he made a promise to Our Lady that he would spend the rest of his life telling families throughout the world how Mary desires to help them and bringing the daily rosary into their homes. In his zeal for spreading the rosary, he became one of the greatest promoters of the rosary in the history of the Church.

After initiating a radio program in Albany, New York, that sought to spread the family rosary, he officially launched the Family Rosary apostolate in 1942. As part of his efforts to spread the family rosary across America, he wrote to every bishop in the United States and asked them to promote the family rosary in their respective dioceses. He coined the catchy slogan, "The family that prays together stays together," and was able to mobilize some of the most famous Hollywood actors and celebrities of his time to support his rosary efforts. He even got many of these celebrities to appear on television programs and radio broadcasts to promote the family rosary. In 1947, he launched Family Theater Productions as a further method for promoting the family rosary through the media, and, in 1948, he began the Family Rosary Crusades apostolate. During his lifetime, he organized rosary events in more than 40 countries, gathering over 28 million people to pray the rosary! He was greatly loved by many popes and was a personal friend of St. Teresa of Calcutta. He is buried in Holy Cross Cemetery, located on the grounds of Stonehill College in Easton, Massachusetts.

Marian Devotion

The fervent Marian devotion of Fr. Patrick Peyton can be traced back to his formative years in Ireland. He was greatly influenced by his devout Catholic parents and the Marian devotion of the Irish people. Every evening, his mother would call the family to prayer, and his father would lead the family rosary in the home.

During his time as a seminarian in the United States, after his healing from tuberculosis took place, his love for Mary turned into an apostolate. He understood his mission in life to be spreading devotion to Mary and her rosary, writing several books and addressing crowds across the world. Mary was his princess. He was honored to bring solid teaching about his princess to every nation, and often referred to himself as "Mary's donkey." The famous actress Loretta Young once made the remark that she had never met a man so in love with a woman as Fr. Peyton was in love with the Blessed Virgin Mary.

His Marian devotion inspired many people all over the world to pray the rosary as a means of peaceful resistance to dictatorial regimes. For example, in 1986, during the People Power Revolution that overthrew the oppressive dictatorship of President Ferdinand Marcos in the Philippines, it was the message of Fr. Patrick Peyton that gave the Filipino people tremendous strength and heroic courage sufficient to enable them to stand in front of armed tanks and pray the rosary. On the famous EDSA freeway, the people were encouraged to stand their ground and pray the rosary when they saw the huge billboards for Fr. Patrick Peyton's Rosary Crusades that lined the street. The billboards read: "The family that prays together stays together" and "A world at prayer is a world at peace." The rosary brought about a peaceful revolution; not a single shot was fired.

Champion of the Rosary

Without exaggeration, the efforts of Fr. Patrick Peyton to spread the family rosary are unparalleled. Truly deserving to be called the rosary priest, he not only founded major movements to promote the family rosary, but also produced 15 short films that used the mysteries of the rosary as their central themes. He was so bold in service to his mission that, in 1971, he wrote a letter to Pope Paul VI requesting the rosary's elevation to the status of a liturgical prayer! He made such a request because he was watching entire nations turn away from the rosary during the 1960s and early 1970s. The rejection of the rosary greatly disturbed him, and he begged the Vicar of Christ to do something about it. The response from Rome came in the form of Bl. Pope Paul VI's famous 1974 apostolic letter *Marialis Cultus.* Though the letter did not elevate the rosary to the status of a liturgical prayer, Bl. Pope Paul VI greatly defended the rosary, encouraged the faithful to pray it, and placed a particular emphasis on the family rosary.

In the mind of Fr. Peyton, the rosary is the Psalter of Redemption because it lovingly intertwines two most beautiful prayers: the Our Father and the Hail Mary. He considered the rosary a method of evangelization and a catechetical tool; for this reason, he always emphasized the importance of reciting the Creed at the beginning of the rosary. Like many others, he expressed a desire for additional mysteries to be associated with the rosary so that people could learn to meditate more frequently on the public life of Jesus. Several of the mysteries he proposed would later be incorporated into the rosary by St. John Paul II. Echoing the words of Bl. Pope Pius IX, Fr. Peyton informed everyone in attendance at his events that when they held the rosary in their hands, they were holding the "single richest treasure in the Vatican." He was convinced that praying the rosary as a family would make virtue and good works flourish in both the home and in society. To further encourage people to pray the rosary, he promoted the 15 promises of Our Lady to those who pray the rosary (see page 210).

Due to the effectiveness and popularity of his Family Rosary Crusades, Fr. Peyton received personal invitations from bishops all around the world to visit their countries and spread the family rosary. In 1961, more than 550,000 people attended his rosary rally in San Francisco. This event was proclaimed by the archdiocesan archivist the most important event in the history of the Archdiocese of San Francisco. In 1962, he gathered more than one million people in Colombia to pray the rosary, and in the same year in Rio de Janeiro, Brazil, he gathered over 1.5 million. In 1964, he gathered 2 million people in Sao Paulo, Brazil, and in 1985, he gathered well over 2 million people in the Philippines to pray the rosary.

Rosary Gems

From my earliest memories, I saw my father with the rosary beads in his hands and my mother holding hers.

~ Servant of God Patrick Peyton

The rosary can bring families through all dangers and evils.

~ Servant of God Patrick Peyton

I want to get ten million families to pray the rosary every day.

~ Servant of God Patrick Peyton

Because of the daily family rosary, my home was for me a cradle, a school, a university, a library, and most of all, a little church.

~ Servant of God Patrick Peyton

It is the rosary prayed by families that will keep the lights of faith glowing in the days of darkness of faith, as it has done in the past.

~ Servant of God Patrick Peyton

Countless families the world over invite Mary to their homes through the family rosary. She comes. They sense her presence. They solve their problems because where Mary is present there is Christ, her Divine Son.

~ Servant of God Patrick Peyton

What a blessed thing it would be if we could pray the rosary over nationwide radio and bring Our Blessed Mother into every home in America.

~ Servant of God Patrick Peyton

We must hold fast to the treasure of the rosary, the gift of Our Blessed Mother.

~ Servant of God Patrick Peyton

We must never forget the rosary and its meaning, the very embodiment of our Christianity.

~ Servant of God Patrick Peyton

Like all the works and events in the Church, the rosary has the power and touch of the Holy Spirit upon it.

~ Servant of God Patrick Peyton

Starting on their wedding day my parents knelt each evening before the hearth to say together the family rosary, that God and Mary might protect and bless their home and fill it with the laughter of children.

~ Servant of God Patrick Peyton

Throughout history the friends of Our Blessed Lady have devised ways and means of asking for her power and intercession, and the most outstanding means is the rosary.

~ Servant of God Patrick Peyton

The one thing I want to do with my life is to devote every minute of it to restoring the family rosary.

~ Servant of God Patrick Peyton

What is so good about the rosary is that it goes all the way in telling the whole story of Jesus and Mary and ourselves.

~ Servant of God Patrick Peyton

It's in that school, in that sanctuary, in that holy home of the rosary, that I discovered Mary! And in discovering Mary, I discovered a protector. I found a friend. I found a mother that would never die. I found a mother filled with affection for me, filled with concern for my welfare, lavishing upon me her strength, her prayers, her guidance, her protection. I'm speaking to you of Mary, the Mother of Jesus Christ. And thanks to the family rosary, this is the greatest fruit that it gave me.

~ Servant of God Patrick Peyton

When combined with the pure contemplative prayer of the rosary meditations, the Hail Mary becomes the most powerful weapon ever placed in the hands of man — a weapon which, through God and his most blessed Mother, will someday change the face of the earth.

~ Servant of God Patrick Peyton

When you look at the rosary in your hand it appears very simple, that little string of beads, yet how far that short chain reaches, what a cosmos it encircles, how closely it binds us to God and to Mary. You hold the power to change your lives.

~ Servant of God Patrick Peyton

BLESSED POPE PAUL VI

The Defender
of the Rosary
1897–1978

PAPACY: 1963–1978
BEATIFIED: October 19, 2014 by Pope Francis with
Pope Emeritus Benedict XVI in attendance
FEAST DAY: September 26

BLESSED POPE PAUL VI was born in northern Italy and elected the Vicar of Christ during the turbulent 1960s and 1970s. Before being elected to the papacy, he had earned a doctorate in canon law and served as the Vatican Secretary of State, as well as the archbishop of Milan. Upon the death of St. Pope John XXIII, the Second Vatican Council was halted, but Bl. Pope Paul VI re-opened it and brought about its conclusion in 1965.

Blessed Pope Paul VI was an extremely humble man. After his death, it became known that, during his papal visit to the Philippines in 1970, he had been stabbed in the chest in the Manila airport by a Bolivian poet and artist who had disguised himself as a priest. The man who stabbed him, Benjamin Mendoza, had purchased a dagger in a Muslim thrift shop. Interestingly, the miracle that was approved for Bl. Pope Paul VI's beatification was worked through the relic of the blood left on his vestment from the stabbing. The case involved an unborn child in his mother's womb that had suffered brain defects during pregnancy. The mother's physician advised her to abort the child, but the mother refused. Instead, she asked for the intercession of Pope Paul VI at the urging of a nun who gave her a holy card with a piece of the pope's cassock from the attack in Manila. When the child was born, to the surprise of everyone, there were no brain defects. Interestingly, it had been Bl. Pope Paul VI who wrote the landmark encyclical *Humanae Vitae* that defended all human life and condemned all forms of artificial birth control. Blessed Pope Paul VI was known as the "pope of firsts" because he was the first pope to ever fly on a plane, the first pope to visit Fatima, and the first pope to visit the Holy Land since St. Peter.

Marian Devotion

Blessed Pope Paul VI's tender devotion to Mary is evident in his request that his first Mass as a priest be celebrated in the Basilica of Santa Maria delle Grazie in Brescia. As a bishop and then later as pope, he frequently spoke at Marian congresses and events in order to encourage devotion to Mary. He considered the Sacrament of Baptism a prolongation of the virginal maternity of Mary and boldly taught that for a person to be a true Christian, they needed to be Marian. In all of his teachings on Mary, he always emphasized that Our Lady is the model of Christian perfection.

Like many of his predecessors, he fervently promoted the month of May as a special time for honoring Mary. He even released an apostolic exhortation titled *Mense Maio* (*The Month of May*) on this subject in 1965. The year 1965 was also the concluding year of the Second Vatican Council. At the end of the Council, Paul VI declared Mary the Mother of the Church. On the 50th anniversary of the apparitions at Fatima (May 13, 1967), he became the first pope to visit Fatima. He visited many Marian shrines during his papacy and wrote the apostolic exhortation *Marialis Cultus* in 1974. This landmark document sought to correct the neglect in Marian devotion that had occurred after the Second Vatican Council. He also beatified the great Franciscan priest and martyr of charity, St. Maximilian Kolbe.

Champion of the Rosary

During the first general audience of his pontificate, Bl. Pope Paul VI extolled praying the rosary as an especially beneficial pious practice for all the faithful. He was very much in favor of the family rosary and spoke about it frequently throughout his papacy. He made frequent reference to the importance of meditation during the rosary, stating that the rosary without contemplation is like a body without a soul. While the Second Vatican Council was taking place, he wrote a letter to the papal legate for the Mariological Congress being held in the Dominican Republic and specifically noted that one of the exercises of Marian piety that the Fathers of the Council were recommending was the rosary. Then, in 1966, one year after the Council, he wrote *Christi Matri*, emphasizing again that the Second Vatican Council had intended to promote the rosary.

In 1967, when he revised the list of indulgences offered by the Church, he simplified the indulgences and limited them to two categories: partial or plenary. The new list contained a section on the rosary and made the indulgences attached to the rosary much easier to understand. In 1969, in honor of the fourth centenary of the document of St. Pope Pius V codifying the form of the rosary, he published the apostolic letter *Recurrens Mensis October* to promote praying the rosary in October and offering the rosary as a means of bringing about peace in the world.

During his pontificate, many theologians wanted him to revise the prayer of the rosary and break from his predecessor's acceptance of the pious tradition of the rosary's origins through St. Dominic. To his perpetual credit, Bl. Pope Paul VI remained staunchly opposed to such ideas. While he understood there had been legitimate adaptations and developments of the rosary over the centuries, he had no intention of changing the rosary or, as many theologians were suggesting he do, rejecting the consensus of his predecessors about the rosary's history. In fact, in the course of preparations for *Marialis Cultus,* his most well-known Marian document, he regularly sent the drafts back to the theological ghostwriters because he did not agree with their attempts to change the rosary or rewrite its history. He did this four times! It was for this reason that *Marialis Cultus* took three years to compose. *Marialis Cultus* was not promulgated until Bl. Pope Paul VI was satisfied with it. He was a staunch defender of the rosary.

Rosary Gems

The rosary is a Gospel prayer.

~ Blessed Pope Paul VI

By its nature the recitation of the rosary calls for a quiet rhythm and a lingering pace, helping the individual to meditate on the mysteries of the Lord's life as seen through the eyes of her who was closest to the Lord.

~ Blessed Pope Paul VI

The succession of Hail Marys [of the rosary] constitutes the warp on which is woven the contemplation of the mysteries.

~ Blessed Pope Paul VI

Meditating on the mysteries of the holy rosary, we learn, after the example of Mary, to have peace in our souls, through the unceasing and loving contact with Jesus and the mysteries of his redemptive life.

~ Blessed Pope Paul VI

The rosary is an exercise of piety that draws its motivating force from the liturgy and leads naturally back to it.

~ Blessed Pope Paul VI

Do not fail to put repeated emphasis on the recitation of the rosary, the prayer so pleasing to Our Lady and so often recommended by the Roman Pontiffs.

~ Blessed Pope Paul VI

We like to think, and sincerely hope, that when the family gathering becomes a time of prayer, the rosary is a frequent and favored manner of praying.

~ Blessed Pope Paul VI

If evils increase, the devotion of the People of God should also increase. And so, venerable brothers [bishops], we want you to take the lead in urging and encouraging people to pray ardently to our most merciful mother Mary by saying the rosary ... this prayer is well-suited to the devotion of the People of God, most pleasing to the Mother of God and most effective in gaining heaven's blessings. The Second Vatican Council recommended use of the rosary to all the sons of the Church, not in express words but in unmistakable fashion in this phrase: "Let them value highly the pious practices and exercises directed to the Blessed Virgin and approved over the centuries by the Magisterium."

~ Blessed Pope Paul VI

The rosary is a devotion that, through the Blessed Mother, leads us to Jesus.

~ Blessed Pope Paul VI

Without contemplation, the rosary is a body without a soul.

~ Blessed Pope Paul VI

As the history of the Church makes clear, this very fruitful way of praying [the rosary] is not only efficacious in warding off evils and preventing calamities, but is also of great help in fostering Christian life.

~ Blessed Pope Paul VI

We now desire, as a continuation of the thought of our predecessors, to recommend strongly the recitation of the family rosary.

~ Blessed Pope Paul VI

We exhort all Catholic families to introduce this devotion [the rosary] into their lives, and to encourage its propagation.

~ Blessed Pope Paul VI

Blessed are we if we are faithful in reciting that very popular and splendid prayer — the rosary — which is a kind of measured spelling out of our feelings of affection in the invocation: Hail Mary, Hail Mary, Hail Mary. Our life will be a fortunate one if it is interwoven with this garland of roses, with this circlet of praise to Mary, to the mysteries of her Divine Son.

~ Blessed Pope Paul VI

VENERABLE FULTON J. SHEEN

The Bishop of the Rosary 1895–1979

V ENERABLE FULTON J. SHEEN was born in El
Paso, Illinois, and is considered one of the first Catholic
televangelists. Archbishop Fulton Sheen was a master orator with
a quick wit and an uncanny ability to present deep theological
topics in a simple and understandable way. The famed G.K. Chesterton greatly admired him and wrote the introduction to Sheen's
first book, published in 1925. As a priest, he reached over 4 million people every Sunday from 1930 to 1952 with his nationally
broadcast radio program "The Catholic Hour." In 1952, he was
made an auxiliary bishop of the Archdiocese of New York and
began a television program called "Life is Worth Living." This
program lasted for five years and, on average, reached over 30
million people every week. The program was so popular that he
won two Emmy awards. Though he held a doctorate in philosophy, his message was understandable by the vast majority of
people and appealed to everyone, including non-Catholics.

Sheen was later made the bishop of Rochester, New York,
and eventually an archbishop. In spite of his busy schedule, he
still found time to write more than 73 books. Deeply devoted to
the Eucharist, he was dedicated to spending a Holy Hour before
the Blessed Sacrament every day, and often remarked that all his
ability to preach and teach came from that daily devotion. He
converted many famous people to Catholicism and served as the
National Director of the Society for the Propagation of the Faith.
Two months before he died, he met St. John Paul II during a
papal visit to St. Patrick's Cathedral in New York City. During that
encounter, St. John Paul II embraced him, praised his work, and
told him that he was a "loyal son of the Church."

Marian Devotion

When Fulton Sheen was born, his mother consecrated him
to the Blessed Virgin Mary. Then, when he received his First Holy
Communion, his mother renewed this consecration. All throughout his youth, Sheen had an intense love for the Blessed Mother.
During his priestly ministry, Mary was a frequent theme of his
sermons, and he often gave inspiring conferences regarding the
role of Mary in the spiritual life. When Sheen became a bishop,
he chose the phrase *Da per matrem me venire* ("That I may come

to you through the Mother") as his episcopal motto. His favorite Marian shrine was Our Lady of Lourdes, which he visited over 30 times throughout his life.

Sheen's eloquence in writing about Our Lady is evidenced in his Marian masterpiece, *The World's First Love: Mary, Mother of God*. In this book, and in many of his other writings, he stressed the central importance of the person of Mary in Christianity, noting that God created his own mother and loved her so much that he gave her 10 times as much of his life as he did his apostles. In other words, Our Blessed Lord gave three years of his life to his disciples, but he gave 30 years to his dear mother. In eloquent prose, Sheen speaks of Mary as the ciborium of the Real Presence, the key to the treasure box that is Jesus, the heart of Christianity, and the one through whom the Muslims will come to Christ. He always emphasized that Jesus and Mary were inseparable, saying that if a person loses the mother, they will eventually also lose the Son.

Champion of the Rosary

As a priest, a bishop, and an archbishop, Fulton Sheen always promoted the rosary. In his numerous philosophical and theological books, he always found a way to fit in a thought or two on the rosary. He firmly believed that the rosary had the power to transform both individuals and society at large. He encouraged people to pray it while walking, working, and driving. In his day, he even noted that the knobs on most steering wheels could be used as counters for the Hail Marys. He considered the rosary to be therapeutic, especially since it is a form of meditative prayer that involves touching the beads of the rosary, caressing the crucifix, and kissing it tenderly.

Sheen taught that the rosary is a prayer for everyone, from the simplest person to the greatest theologian. He often reminded those who considered themselves intellectually elite that they were depriving themselves of great graces if they failed to humble themselves and pray the rosary. From 1950 to 1966, he served as the National Director for the Society for the Propagation of the Faith. In that position, he greatly promoted the rosary in a number of ways, including his creation of the World Mission Rosary. His desire was for everyone to make a prayerful missionary tour of the world by praying a rosary made up of different colors signifying the different geographical regions of the world: Green stands for Africa; blue for the vast Pacific region of Oceania; white for Europe; red for the Americas; and yellow for Asia, since it is the land of the rising sun. His World Mission Rosary became very popular and is still in use today.

Rosary Gems

It is objected that there is much repetition in the rosary inasmuch as the Lord's Prayer and the Hail Mary are said so often; therefore it is monotonous. That reminds me of a woman who came to see me one evening after instructions. She said, "I would never become a Catholic. You say the same words in the rosary over and over again, and anyone who repeats the same words is never sincere. I would never believe anyone who repeated his words, and neither would God." I asked her who the man was with her. She said he was her fiancé. I asked: "Does he love you?" "Certainly, he does." "But how do you know?" "He told me." "What did he say?" "He said: 'I love you.'" "When did he tell you last?" "About an hour ago." "Did he tell you before?" "Yes, last night. He tells me every night." I said: "Don't believe him. He is repeating; he is not sincere."

~ Venerable Fulton J. Sheen

In the rosary, we not only say prayers, we think them.

~ Venerable Fulton J. Sheen

Airplanes must have runways before they can fly. What the runway is to the airplane, that the rosary beads are to prayer — the physical start to gain spiritual altitude.

~ Venerable Fulton J. Sheen

No normal mind yet has been overcome by worries or fears who was faithful to the rosary. You will be surprised how you can climb out of your worries, bead by bead, up to the very throne of the Heart of Love itself.

~ Venerable Fulton J. Sheen

Because the rosary is both a mental and a vocal prayer, it is one where intellectual elephants may bathe, and the simple birds may also sip.

~ Venerable Fulton J. Sheen

If you wish to convert anyone to the fullness of the knowledge of Our Lord and of his Mystical Body, then teach him the rosary. One of two things will happen. Either he will stop saying the rosary — or he will get the gift of faith.

~ Venerable Fulton J. Sheen

The beauty of the rosary is that it is not merely a vocal prayer. It is also a mental prayer. One sometimes hears a dramatic presentation in which, while the human voice is speaking, there is a background of beautiful music, giving force and dignity to the words. The rosary is like that.

~ Venerable Fulton J. Sheen

The rosary is the book of the blind, where souls see and there enact the greatest drama of love the world has ever known; it is the book of the simple, which initiates them into mysteries and knowledge more satisfying than the education of other men; it is the book of the aged, whose eyes close upon the shadow of this world and open on the substance of the next.

~ Venerable Fulton J. Sheen

Concentration is impossible when the mind is troubled; thoughts run helter-skelter; a thousand and one images flood across the mind; distracted and wayward, the spiritual seems a long way off. The rosary is the best therapy for these distraught, unhappy, fearful, and frustrated souls, precisely because it involves the simultaneous use of three powers: the physical, the vocal, and the spiritual, and in that order.

~ Venerable Fulton J. Sheen

All the idle moments of one's life can be sanctified, thanks to the rosary. As we walk the streets, we pray with the rosary hidden in our hand or in our pocket; as we are driving an automobile, the little knobs under most steering wheels can serve as counters for the decades. While waiting to be served at a lunchroom, or waiting for a train, or in a store, or while playing dummy at bridge, or when conversation or a lecture lags — all these moments can be sanctified and made to serve inner peace, thanks to a prayer that enables one to pray at all times and under all circumstances.

~ Venerable Fulton J. Sheen

As the magnifying glass catches and unites the scattered rays of the sun, so the rosary brings together the otherwise dissipated thoughts of life in the sickroom into the white and burning heat of Divine Love.

~ Venerable Fulton J. Sheen

In moments when fever, agony, and pain make it hard to pray, the suggestion of prayer that comes from merely holding the rosary — or better still, from caressing the Crucifix at the end of it — is tremendous.

~ Venerable Fulton J. Sheen

The power of the rosary is beyond description.

~ Venerable Fulton J. Sheen

The mind is infinitely variable in its language, but the heart is not. The heart of a man, in the face of the woman he loves, is too poor to translate the infinity of his affection into a different word. So the heart takes one expression, "I love you," and in saying it over and over again, it never repeats. That is what we do when we say the rosary — we are saying to God, the Trinity, to the Incarnate Savior, to the Blessed Mother: "I love you, I love you, I love you."

~ Venerable Fulton J. Sheen

The rosary is a great test of faith. What the Eucharist is in the order of sacraments, that the rosary is in order of sacramental — the mystery and the test of faith, the touchstone by which the soul is judged in its humility. The mark of the Christian is the willingness to look for the Divine in the flesh of a babe in a crib, the continuing Christ under the appearance of bread on an altar, and a meditation and a prayer on a string of beads.

~ Venerable Fulton J. Sheen

ST. TERESA OF CALCUTTA

The Missionary of the Rosary
1910–1997

BEATIFIED: October 19, 2003 by St. John Paul II
CANONIZED: September 4, 2016 by Pope Francis
FEAST DAY: September 5

S AINT TERESA OF CALCUTTA was born in Albania and entered the Sisters of Loreto at the age of 18. While living in India, she witnessed the extreme poverty of many people and was inspired to found a new religious community, the Missionaries of Charity. Her greatest desire was to quench the thirst of Jesus in the destitute, abandoned, and the poorest of the poor around the world. Affectionately known as Mother Teresa, she founded orphanages and homes all around the world that are run by her Missionaries of Charity. In 1979, she was honored with the Nobel Peace Prize.

A woman of deep prayer, St. Teresa lived an intensely Eucharistic spirituality. Incredibly, it was revealed after her death that for most of her life she had experienced long periods of dryness in the spiritual life, lengthy absences of any spiritual consolation, and the dark night of the soul. Nevertheless, all throughout her torturous spiritual dryness, she remained joyful and steadfast in her service to Jesus in the poor. Her witness of trust and selfless service to God and neighbor were extremely inspiring. She was greatly loved by many popes, especially St. John Paul II.

Marian Devotion

As a young girl, St. Teresa made an annual pilgrimage with her mother to the mountain Shrine of Our Lady of Cernagore. The annual pilgrimage made a deep impression on her young heart; she later attested that the annual visits to the shrine of Our Lady helped her respond to her religious vocation. Saint Teresa delighted in visiting Marian shrines throughout her life. She had a particular love for Guadalupe and Our Lady of Fatima, and fervently prayed for the conversion of Russia, as Our Lady requested at Fatima.

Saint Teresa had a tremendous devotion to the Immaculate Heart of Mary, as well as the Miraculous Medal. Everywhere she went, she handed out Miraculous Medals to those who were in attendance at her events. In order to carry out this practice, she asked people to obtain large quantities of Miraculous Medals and give them to her in bags so that she could hand them out during her missionary travels. One of her favorite prayers to Our Lady was the *Memorare;* she was known to stop everything in difficult situations and ask others to pray it with her. Her habit of praying nine *Memorares* in a row for immediate assistance from heaven in a difficult situation became known as the "express novena." She had a boundless trust in Our Lady and sought to imitate Mary's virtues, especially her silent and selfless co-redemptive suffering.

Champion of the Rosary

As a young girl, in addition to making the annual Marian pilgrimage, Teresa also belonged to a Marian sodality at her local parish. This sodality instilled in her a life-long love for the rosary. The rosary became her favorite Marian devotion. Before she founded the Missionaries of Charity, the Blessed Virgin spoke to her and instructed her to teach the rosary to little children and the poor. As was her practice with the Miraculous Medal, she almost always had the rosary in her hand and would pray it at various times throughout the day. She considered holding the rosary to be like holding Mary's hand. The rosary was her constant companion and gave her strength during her years of spiritual dryness and interior suffering.

A true champion of the rosary, St. Teresa required the sisters in all the houses of the Missionaries of Charity around the world to pray the rosary in common every day. Observing the Missionaries of Charity praying the rosary in their chapels is an extremely edifying experience, especially since they pray it with great devotion and without the assistance of kneelers. Saint Teresa's own feet were very worn down and her toes twisted from years of kneeling to pray the rosary on hard floors with no kneelers. In her zeal for the rosary, she declared that she wanted to open 15 convents in Russia in honor of the 15 mysteries of the rosary. (This was before St. John Paul II established the Luminous Mysteries.) Providentially, she ended up opening 20 convents in Russia, even though she had no idea that St. John Paul II would add five more mysteries to the rosary five years after her death!

Once, while she was traveling through an airport in a country plagued with war, everyone in line was asked if they had any weapons on their person. To everyone's surprise, Mother Teresa declared that she had a weapon! She gently opened her wrinkled hand and revealed her weapon to everyone: her rosary.

She was a great admirer of the efforts of Fr. Patrick Peyton to spread the family rosary and attended his events on several occasions to show her support. When she died in 1997, her body was placed in a casket with a rosary and a large Miraculous Medal in her hands.

Rosary Gems

Take care of them — they are mine. Bring them to Jesus — carry Jesus to them. Fear not. Teach them to say the rosary — the family rosary, and all will be well.

~ Our Lady's words to St. Teresa of Calcutta

When we walk the streets, in whatever part of the world, the sisters [Missionaries of Charity] carry in their hands the crown of the rosary. The Virgin is our strength and our protection.

~ St. Teresa of Calcutta

Our [Missionaries of Charity's] holy hour is our daily family prayer where we get together and pray the rosary before the exposed Blessed Sacrament the first half hour, and the second half hour we pray in silence.

~ St. Teresa of Calcutta

We are taught to love and say the rosary with great devotion; let us be very faithful to this our first love — for it will bring us closer to our Heavenly Mother. Our [Missionaries of Charity's] rule asks of us never to go to the slums without first having recited the Mother's praises; that is why we have to say the rosary in the streets and dark holes of the slums. Cling to the rosary as the creeper clings to the tree — for without Our Lady we cannot stand.

~ St. Teresa of Calcutta

The other day I can't tell you how bad I felt — there was a moment when I nearly refused to accept — deliberately I took the rosary and very slowly without even meditating or thinking — I said it slowly and calmly — the moment passed — but the darkness is so dark, and the pain is so painful — but I accept whatever he [Jesus] gives and I give whatever he takes.

~ St. Teresa of Calcutta

We honor her [Mary] by praying the rosary with love and devotion and by radiating her humility, kindness, and thoughtfulness towards others.

~ St. Teresa of Calcutta

Do you pray the rosary often?

~ St. Teresa of Calcutta

Pray the rosary every day.

~ St. Teresa of Calcutta

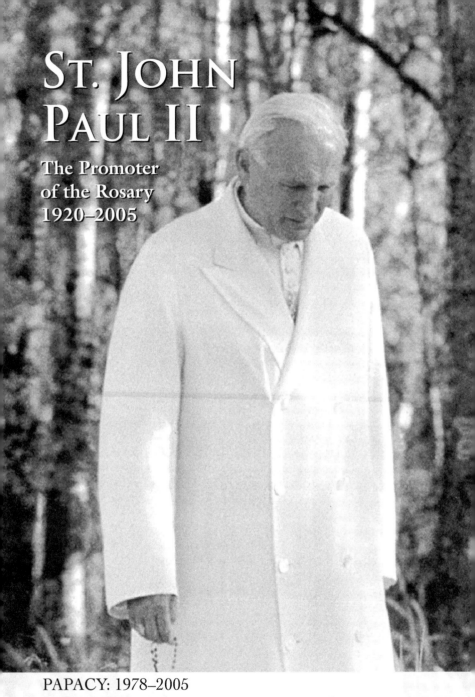

St. John Paul II

The Promoter
of the Rosary
1920–2005

PAPACY: 1978–2005
BEATIFIED: May 1, 2011 by Pope Benedict XVI
CANONIZED: April 27, 2014 by Pope Francis with
Pope Emeritus Benedict XVI in attendance
FEAST DAY: October 22

SAINT JOHN PAUL II was born in Wadowice, Poland, and became the first non-Italian pope since the 16ᵗʰ century. As a young man, he was an actor and an avid skier, kayaker, and outdoorsman. He grew up in a very difficult time under the Nazi and Communist occupations of Poland, which forced him to study to become a priest in secret. An extremely intelligent and erudite man, he was sent to Rome after his ordination and studied under some of the greatest theologians of his time. He never lost his love for the outdoors and was out kayaking on the day the news arrived that Venerable Pope Pius XII had selected him to be an auxiliary bishop. He knew at least 12 languages, was eventually made the archbishop of Krakow, and was a participant at the Second Vatican Council.

He was elected to be the Vicar of Christ in 1978, and quickly became one of the most influential popes in the history of the Church. He brought the Church out of the turbulent 1960s and 1970s, helped end Communism in Europe, visited 129 countries, beatified 1,338 people, and canonized 482 saints. He wrote 14 encyclicals, 15 apostolic exhortations, and 45 apostolic letters. He was also an apostle of the Divine Mercy message and devotion as given to St. Faustina Kowalska, established Divine Mercy Sunday, and offered groundbreaking teaching on topics such as the theology of the body.

On May 13, 1981, the anniversary of the first apparition of Our Lady at Fatima, John Paul II was shot in St. Peter's Square by the radical Turkish Muslim Mehmet Ali Agca. It was later reported that just before St. John Paul II was shot, he had made a slight movement toward a little girl who was holding a holy card of Our Lady of Fatima. Our Lady of Fatima saved him on that day, and he knew it. On October 7 of that same year, the Feast of Our Lady of the Rosary and his first general public audience after his recovery, he made reference to the connection between being shot on May 13 and the Fatima apparitions. Incredibly, a second assassination attempt was made one year later on May 12, 1982, in Fatima itself. During his pilgrimage to Fatima in thanksgiving to Our Lady for having saved his life from the previous year's assassination attempt, a Catholic priest from the Society of St. Pius X, Fr. Juan María Fernández Krohn, attempted to kill St.

John Paul II. This mentally disturbed clergyman tried to stab St. John Paul II with a bayonet, but failed. Our Lady of Fatima had saved him again. Then, in 1995, an Al-Qaeda-funded attempt to kill the pope by means of a suicide bomber was foiled one week before its execution while Pope John Paul II was on a trip to the Philippines for World Youth Day. Mary's mantle was over St. John Paul II.

He would live for 10 more years before dying on the vigil of Divine Mercy Sunday in 2005. For his holiness and monumental apostolic activity, St. John Paul II rightly deserves to be known as St. John Paul the Great.

Marian Devotion

Karol Wojtyła had a filial love for Mary. After losing his earthly mother at a very early age, he entrusted himself to Our Lady's care and had complete confidence in her. He was greatly influenced by the Marian writings of St. Louis de Montfort and said that reading *True Devotion to the Blessed Virgin* was a turning point in his life. In fact, when he was elected the Vicar of Christ, he chose as his pontifical motto a Marian phrase from the writings of St. Louis de Montfort: "*Totus Tuus*," that is, "All Yours [Mary]." In his frequent catechetical talks on Mary and her maternal role in Christianity, he emphasized that it is impossible for people to understand the Church unless they look to Mary, since there is no other person who can better introduce us to the knowledge of Christ than his mother.

Saint John Paul II promoted the Marian Sodality and the Legion of Mary everywhere he went. In his many world travels as pope, he greatly delighted in visiting Marian shrines. During many of these visits, St. John Paul II took the opportunity to speak of Our Lady as our maternal Mediatrix, the masterpiece of God's mercy, the pattern of Christian holiness, and the woman of the Eucharist who leads her spiritual children to the Real Presence of Christ. He encouraged all the members of the Church, especially youth, to foster a filial devotion to Mary, and led by example by bringing Our Lady into everything he said and did.

When he was shot in 1981, during the surgery to remove the bullet, he requested that the doctors not remove his Brown

Scapular. During his convalescence in the Gemelli Clinic in Rome, he asked for two things: the secret that Mary had given to the children of Fatima and the *Diary* of St. Faustina Kowalska. In 1984, a few years after his full recovery, he consecrated the world to the Immaculate Heart. According to the Servant of God Lúcia Dos Santos, St. John Paul II's consecration fulfilled Mary's request at Fatima that the world, including Russia, be consecrated to her Immaculate Heart. A few years after the consecration, he declared a Marian Year that was observed from 1987 to 1988 and published the Marian encyclical *Redemptoris Mater.* It was shortly after these events that the USSR fell apart and Communism ended in Russia.

Champion of the Rosary

Saint John Paul II's tremendous love of the rosary can be traced to his young adult years in Poland. Beginning in 1940, Karol Wojtyła attended a weekly Living Rosary group started by the Servant of God Jan Tyranowski. In this group, each member was given a particular mystery to meditate on for one month, saying a decade a day while contemplating that particular mystery. It was during this time in Wojtyła's life that Jan Tyranowski suggested he read St. Louis de Montfort's *True Devotion to the Blessed Virgin.* Tyranowski's example of Marian devotion was a major influence on Wojtyła; quite a few historians have noted that had it not been for Tyranowski, Wojtyła might not have become a priest. As a newly ordained priest, Fr. Wojtyła started a Living Rosary group for the youth at his first parish in 1948. In 1996, Pope John Paul II recalled the memory of his friend and Marian mentor Jan Tyranowski, calling him a "great apostle of the Living Rosary." As a priest, bishop, cardinal, and pope, St. John Paul II was also a great apostle of the rosary.

As a bishop in Krakow, he was known to pay regular visits to Kalvaria Zebrzydowska, the principal Marian shrine of the Archdiocese of Krakow. During these visits, he would walk along the paths praying his rosary. During the winter, when there was snow or ice on the ground, he would clasp a ski pole in one hand and a rosary in the other as he walked the grounds of the shrine. Today, there is a statue of St. John Paul II holding a rosary in his hand in front of this Marian shrine. As a cardinal, he was invited to the

Vatican by Bl. Pope Paul VI in 1976 to give a Lenten retreat and affirmed his devotion to the rosary by choosing the rosary and its mysteries as his main theme.

After his election to the papacy on October 16, 1978, it only took him two weeks to announce to the world that the rosary was his favorite prayer (October 29, 1978). He even stated on that same day that the rosary was a prayer-commentary on *Lumen Gentium*, the document from the Second Vatican Council that included a chapter on Mary. For the duration of his pontificate, rarely a year went by in which he did not do something monumental to promote the rosary. On March 3, 1979, he began the practice of praying the rosary over Vatican Radio on the First Saturday of each month. On October 21, 1979, he visited the Shrine of Our Lady of Pompeii, and in 1980, he beatified the great apostle of the rosary Bartolo Longo. In 1981, he promoted the family rosary in the apostolic exhortation *Familiaris Consortio*, and in 1982, he visited the resting place of St. Dominic in Bologna.

Among the many other significant rosary events of his papacy, two in particular stand out. First, on September 19, 1996, he went to Saint-Laurent-sur-Sèvre, France, and prayed at the tomb of St. Louis de Montfort. Second, in 2002, he wrote the apostolic letter *Rosarium Virginis Mariae*, in which he gave the Church the Luminous Mysteries and declared that, from October 7, 2002, to October 7, 2003, the Church would celebrate a Year of the Rosary. He himself closed out the Year of the Rosary by making another visit to the Shrine of Our Lady of the Rosary in Pompeii.

Saint John Paul II was the most traveled pope in history and brought the rosary with him everywhere he went. He gave out rosaries at all of his papal audiences, encouraged young people at World Youth Days to pray it, and gave the edifying example of praying the entire rosary every day. He asked all people to promote the rosary with fervor and conviction, and taught that the rosary is among the finest and most praiseworthy methods of Christian contemplation. His gift to the Church of the Luminous Mysteries of the rosary was a means of "re-sharpening" or "re-loading" the spiritual weapon of the rosary.

Rosary Gems

The rosary is my favorite prayer.

~ St. John Paul II

The holy rosary introduces us into the very heart of faith. With our thoughts fixed on it, we greet repeatedly, joyfully, the holy Mother of God; declare blessed the Son, the sweet fruit of her womb; and invoke her motherly protection in life and in death.

~ St. John Paul II

The rosary, though clearly Marian in character, is at heart a Christocentric prayer.

~ St. John Paul II

How could one possibly contemplate the mystery of the Child in Bethlehem, in the joyful mysteries [of the rosary], without experiencing the desire to welcome, defend and promote life, and to shoulder the burdens of suffering children all over the world?

~ St. John Paul II

With the rosary, the Christian people sit at the school of Mary.

~ St. John Paul II

She [Mary] prays with us. The rosary prayer embraces the problems of the Church, of the See of St. Peter, and the problems of the whole world.

~ St. John Paul II

To recite the rosary is nothing other than to contemplate with Mary the face of Christ.

~ St. John Paul II

It [the rosary] shows, through the vicissitudes of the Son of God and of the Virgin, how constant in human life is the alteration of good and evil, calm and storms, joyful days and sad ones.

~ St. John Paul II

The rosary, reclaimed in its full meaning, goes to the heart of Christian life.

~ St. John Paul II

If properly revitalized, the rosary is an aid and certainly not a hindrance to ecumenism!

~ St. John Paul II

The repetition of the Hail Mary in the rosary gives us a share in God's own wonder and pleasure: in jubilant amazement we acknowledge the greatest miracle in history.

~ St. John Paul II

The rosary belongs among the finest and most praiseworthy traditions of Christian contemplation.

~ St. John Paul II

Daily recitation of the rosary in the family was once widespread. How worthwhile would such a practice be today! Mary's rosary removes the seeds of family breakup; it is the sure bond of communion and peace.

~ St. John Paul II

The family that prays together stays together. The holy rosary, by age-old tradition, has shown itself particularly effective as a prayer which brings the family together. Individual family members, in turning their eyes toward Jesus, also regain the ability to look one another in the eye, to communicate, to show solidarity, to forgive one another and to see their covenant of love renewed in the Spirit of God.

~ St. John Paul II

To return to the recitation of the family rosary means filling daily life with very different images, images of the mystery of salvation: the image of the Redeemer, the image of his most Blessed Mother. The family that recites the rosary together reproduces something of the atmosphere of the household of Nazareth: its members place Jesus at the center.

~ St. John Paul II

To pray the rosary is to hand over our burdens to the merciful hearts of Christ and his Mother.

~ St. John Paul II

To understand the rosary, one has to enter into the psychological dynamic proper to love.

~ St. John Paul II

The rosary can be recited in full every day, and there are those who most laudably do so.

~ St. John Paul II

At times when Christianity itself seemed under threat, its deliverance was attributed to the power of this prayer [the rosary], and Our Lady of the Rosary was acclaimed as the one whose intercession brought salvation.

~ St. John Paul II

In the present international situation, I appeal to all — individuals, families and communities — to pray the rosary for peace, even daily, so that the world will be preserved from the dreadful scourge of terrorism.

~ St. John Paul II

We must be strong and prepared and trust in Christ and in his Holy Mother and be very, very assiduous in praying the holy rosary.

~ St. John Paul II

Dear brothers and sisters, recite the rosary every day. I earnestly urge Pastors to pray the rosary and to teach people in the Christian communities how to pray it. For the faithful and courageous fulfillment of the human and Christian duties proper to each one's state, help the people of God to return to the daily recitation of the rosary.

~ St. John Paul II

The rosary mystically transports us to Mary's side as she is busy watching over the human growth of Christ in the home of Nazareth.

~ St. John Paul II

The history of the rosary shows how this prayer was used in particular by the Dominicans at a difficult time for the Church due to the spread of heresy. Today we are facing new challenges. Why should we not once more have recourse to the rosary, with the same faith as those who have gone before us?

~ St. John Paul II

[Saint] Joseph Vaz was on fire with faith. Guided by the example of his Divine Master, he travelled the whole island [of Sri Lanka], going everywhere, often barefoot, with a rosary round his neck as a sign of his Catholic faith.

~ St. John Paul II

To recite the rosary means to learn to gaze on Jesus with his Mother's eyes, and to love Jesus with his Mother's heart. Today, my dear young people, I am also, in spirit, handing you the rosary beads. Through prayer and meditation on the mysteries, Mary leads you safely towards her Son! Do not be ashamed to recite the rosary alone, while you walk along the streets to school, to the university or to work, or as you commute by public transport. Adopt the habit of reciting it among yourselves, in your groups, movements and associations. Do not hesitate to suggest that it be recited at home by your parents and brothers and sisters, because it rekindles and strengthens the bonds between family members. This prayer will help you to be strong in your faith, constant in charity, joyful and persevering in hope.

~ St. John Paul II

Confidently take up the rosary once again. Rediscover the rosary in light of Scripture, in harmony with the liturgy, and in the context of your daily lives. May this appeal of mine not go unheard!

~ St. John Paul II

Our beloved John Paul II was a great Apostle of the Rosary: we remember him on his knees, his rosary beads in his hands, immersed in the contemplation of Christ.

~ Pope Benedict XVI

POPE BENEDICT XVI

The Theologian
of the Rosary
1927–present

PAPACY: 2005–2013

POPE BENEDICT XVI was born in Bavaria, Germany, and is one of the most brilliant men to ever hold the office of pope. Before being elected to the papacy, he was an accomplished pianist, an academic theologian who served as a theological consultant at the Second Vatican Council, and the archbishop of Munich and Freising. During his many years of living in Rome, he held the offices of prefect for the Congregation of the Doctrine of the Faith, dean of the College of Cardinals, president of the International Theological Commission, and president of the Pontifical Biblical Commission. He was elected to the papacy in 2005.

In 2013, due to poor health and old age, Pope Benedict XVI resigned from the papacy, making way for a younger and healthier pontiff to hold the office of the Vicar of Christ. After his resignation, he continued to live in the Vatican and serve the Church through a life of prayer under the title "Pope Emeritus Benedict XVI." He is the first pope to relinquish the office of the papacy since Pope Gregory XII in 1415. Many of his theological works are recognized as spiritual classics.

Marian Devotion

The Marian devotion of Pope Benedict XVI is deeply rooted in a biblical, liturgical, and ecclesial approach to Our Lady. He emphasized in both his Marian devotion and his theological writings on Mary that, from a biblical perspective, she is best understood as the Daughter of Zion, the mother of the Messiah, and our spiritual mother. He also emphasized her relationship to God as the Spouse of the Holy Spirit, which allows her to more deeply fulfill her role as our spiritual mother by bringing the Holy Spirit with her wherever she is present.

Pope Benedict XVI also has a rich liturgical Marian devotion. He delighted in emphasizing that the month of May was to be a time particularly devoted to Mary, and he always stressed that the liturgical season of Advent should be understood as a Marian season because it is in Advent that we await the coming of Jesus through Mary. Like previous popes, he, too, loved to visit Marian shrines. In 2008, he made a special pilgrimage to Lourdes to celebrate the 150th anniversary of the Lourdes apparitions.

The Marian dimension of the Church is where Pope Benedict XVI's devotion to Mary has shone most plainly. He depicts the Church as a Marian mystery and shows that Our Lady has an absolutely necessary role in carrying out the providential plan of God in Christ. Mary serves as the archetype, mirror, and truest image of the Church and the Christian. She is the driving force of catholicity and the person the members of the Church must look to in order to truly understand the truth about Jesus Christ, the Church, and ourselves. He taught that if the Church were to fall silent in her praise and devotion to Mary, the Church itself would no longer be capable of glorifying God as she ought, since the Bible itself teaches the praises of Mary. In the person of Mary, the Church has a maternal protector and intercessor before the throne of the Almighty.

Champion of the Rosary

As a young boy, Pope Benedict XVI witnessed the tender love his parents had for Our Lady and her rosary. His parents would often gather the entire family together to pray the rosary. Every year during the month of May, the entire family went to Church every day to pray the rosary. This youthful love of the rosary carried into his priestly and academic endeavors. As a cardinal, even though he was entrusted with many responsibilities, he would always find time to pray at least a few decades a day. At times, he would even divide up a specific set of mysteries and intersperse the various mysteries throughout his day. When he became pope, he began to pray the rosary every day, sometimes praying it in the morning or in the evening while walking through the Vatican gardens.

To Pope Benedict, praying the rosary is a pilgrimage since the meditations require a person to make mental visits to the holy places associated with the lives of Jesus and Mary. For this reason, whenever he beatified or canonized a person, he delighted in making reference to their devotion to the rosary and how it helped them to become holy as they made their pilgrimage of faith. He was a very humble pope who rarely talked about himself or his personal Marian devotion; rather, he highlighted the Marian devotion of the saints, especially their love for the rosary.

He is responsible for canonizing the 14th century rosary promoter St. Nuno Álvares Pereira. Like St. Nuno, he knew that the rosary is a weapon and encouraged everyone, especially the youth, to pray it daily.

Throughout his pontificate, and even after his resignation, Pope Benedict XVI has promoted the rosary. In May of 2008, he led the rosary on the First Saturday of the month in the Basilica of Santa Maria Maggiore in Rome. In October of the same year, he visited the Shrine of Our Lady of the Rosary in Pompeii and spoke very highly of Bl. Bartolo Longo and all that he did to promote the rosary. In May of 2010, he visited Fatima and prayed the rosary publicly with those present. Also in 2010, when 33 Chilean miners were trapped deep in an underground mine for 69 days, he blessed 33 rosaries in Rome and sent them to the trapped miners. The rosaries were sent down the narrow shaft to the miners, who began to pray the rosary every day and wore the blessed rosaries around their necks. Miraculously, all 33 men survived and were rescued on October 13, the anniversary of the Miracle of the Sun at Fatima, where Our Lady appeared under the title "Our Lady of the Rosary!" During the Year of Faith (2012-2013) he asked all Catholics, especially families, to rediscover the prayer of the rosary and to pray it. On August 28, 2014, one year after he resigned from the papacy, a group of Cuban bishops were visiting the Vatican for the installation of an image of Our Lady of Cobre in the Vatican gardens, and were personally invited by Pope Emeritus Benedict XVI to join him later that evening in the Vatican gardens to pray the rosary.

Rosary Gems

The traditional image of Our Lady of the Rosary portrays Mary who with one arm supports the Child Jesus and with the other is offering the rosary beads to St. Dominic. This important iconography shows that the rosary is a means given by the Virgin to contemplate Jesus and, in meditating on his life, to love him and follow him ever more faithfully.

~ Pope Benedict XVI

The recitation of the rosary allows us to fix our gaze and our hearts upon Jesus, just like his Mother, the supreme model of contemplation of the Son.

~ Pope Benedict XVI

I urge you all to recite the rosary every day, abandoning yourselves with trust in Mary's hands.

~ Pope Benedict XVI

The rosary is the prayer of the Christian who advances in the pilgrimage of faith, in the following of Jesus, preceded by Mary.

~ Pope Benedict XVI

Today, together we confirm that the holy rosary is not a pious practice banished to the past, like prayers of other times thought of with nostalgia. Instead, the rosary is experiencing a new springtime. Without a doubt, this is one of the most eloquent signs of love that the young generation nourishes for Jesus and his Mother, Mary.

~ Pope Benedict XVI

Our Lady invites us every year to rediscover the beauty of this prayer [the rosary], so simple and so profound.

~ Pope Benedict XVI

Through the rosary we allow ourselves to be guided by Mary, the model of faith, in meditating on the mysteries of Christ. Day after day she helps us to assimilate the Gospel, so that it gives a form to our life as a whole.

~ Pope Benedict XVI

The prayer of the rosary, so dear to [St.] Bernadette and to Lourdes pilgrims, concentrates within itself the depths of the Gospel message. It introduces us to contemplation of the face of Christ. From this prayer of the humble, we can draw an abundance of graces.

~ Pope Benedict XVI

St. Józef Bilczewski was a man of prayer. The Holy Mass, the Liturgy of the Hours, meditation, the rosary and other pious practices formed part of his daily life.

~ Pope Benedict XVI

His [Bl. Ceferino Giménez Malla's] deep religious sense was expressed in his daily participation in Holy Mass and in the recitation of the rosary. The rosary beads themselves, which he always kept in his pocket became the cause of his arrest and made Bl. Ceferino an authentic "martyr of the rosary," because he did not let anyone take the rosary from him, not even when he was at the point of death.

~ Pope Benedict XVI

In the 19th century she [Bl. Anna Maria Adorni] was an exemplary wife and mother and then, widowed, she devoted herself to charity to women in prison and in difficulty, for whose service she founded two religious Institutes. Because of her ceaseless prayer, Mother Adorni was known as the "Living Rosary."

~ Pope Benedict XVI

The rosary is a spiritual weapon in the battle against evil, against all violence, for peace in hearts, in families, in society and in the world.

~ Pope Benedict XVI

Spiritually unite yourselves to Jesus Crucified and trustfully abandon yourselves into the hands of Mary, calling upon her unceasingly with the rosary.

~ Pope Benedict XVI

The historical origin of the rosary lies in the Middle Ages. This was a time when the Psalms were the normal form of prayer. But the great number of unlettered persons of that period could not take part in the biblical Psalms. Therefore people looked for some kind of Psalter for them and found the prayers to Mary with the mysteries of the life of Jesus Christ, strung out like beads on a necklace.

~ Pope Benedict XVI

[Saint] Dominic was canonized in 1234 and it is he himself who, with his holiness, points out to us two indispensable means for making apostolic action effective. In the very first place is Marian devotion which he fostered tenderly and left as a precious legacy to his spiritual sons who, in the history of the Church, have had the great merit of disseminating the prayer of the holy rosary, so dear to the Christian people and so rich in Gospel values: a true school of faith and piety. In the second place, Dominic, who cared for several women's monasteries in France and in Rome, believed unquestioningly in the value of prayers of intercession for the success of the apostolic work.

~ Pope Benedict XVI

HOW TO
CHAMPION THE
ROSARY

Blessed be the Lord my rock, who trains my hands for war, and my fingers for battle.

~ Psalm 144:1

Though we live in the world we are not carrying on a worldly war, for the weapons of our warfare are not worldly but have divine power to destroy strongholds.

~ 2 Corinthians 10:3-4

For the word of God is living and active, sharper than any two-edged sword, piercing to the division of soul and spirit, of joints and marrow, and discerning the thoughts and intentions of the heart.

~ Hebrews 4:12

How to Become a Champion of the Rosary

To be a champion of the rosary, it is not necessary to write books on the rosary or give conferences about it. All that is needed is a heart docile to the Holy Spirit and a desire to make the rosary more known. Here are three simple methods that allow anyone to become a champion of the rosary:

1) Pray the rosary

During a papal visit to the Shrine of Our Lady of the Rosary of Pompeii, Pope Benedict XVI provided the following understanding of what is required in order to become a champion of the rosary. He stated:

> To be apostles of the rosary it is necessary to experience personally the beauty and depth of this prayer which is simple and accessible to everyone. It is first of all necessary to let the Blessed Virgin Mary take one by the hand to contemplate the Face of Christ: a joyful, luminous, sorrowful and glorious face.[1]

In other words, a person cannot give what a person does not have. Thus, it is first necessary for a person to pray the rosary himself; only then can he truly and effectively became an apostle and champion of the rosary. It is from personal experience and a love for the rosary that champions and apostles of the rosary are born.

In becoming a champion of the rosary, it is important to remember that praying the rosary is not about experiencing good feelings. Many times, as in any relationship, pleasant feelings come and go. What determines one's faithfulness in any relationship is perseverance through the difficult and dry times. Champions of the rosary are made when a soul perseveres in praying the rosary, no matter what. Love endures dryness and is consistent in all seasons of life, whether those seasons are joyful, luminous, sorrowful, or glorious. Saint Louis de Montfort knew this and noted the following about persevering in praying the rosary:

> Even if you suffer from dryness of soul, boredom and interior discouragement, never give up even the least little bit of your rosary. On the contrary, like a real champion of Jesus and Mary, you should say your Our Fathers and Hail Marys quite drily if you have to, without seeing, hearing or feeling any consolation whatsoever, and concentrating as best you can on the mysteries.[2]

True champions of the rosary never give up!

2) Encourage others to pray the rosary

It is only natural that after having experienced the power of the rosary to conquer evil, you would desire to hand on the great spiritual sword to another. Like St. Louis de Montfort, we should want to tell the whole world about the great secret of the rosary so that they, too, might tap into its power. A champion of the rosary will have at his disposal a plethora of means to spread the devotion of the rosary to others, such as praying for others to be lit on fire with the same burning love for Our Lady and her rosary as the great champions of the rosary, as well as sharing rosary beads and giving away good books on the rosary to family members, friends, godchildren, fellow parishioners, and co-workers. Many saints followed this last method of spreading the rosary through sharing good books. Blessed James Alberione had these encouraging words to say about how to promote the rosary:

> Make Mary known and loved by others. Invite all to go to Mary. Where Mary enters, Jesus follows. Through Mary to Jesus. Foster the recitation of the rosary in every family. The fruits will be numberless, and we will be able to count them only in heaven. Diffuse books and pamphlets on the rosary; speak of this devotion; exhort its recitation on all good occasions which present themselves. Also give the example: the rosary

witnesses to itself. One who sees the rosary beads in the hands of another will feel the desire to do the same, will receive a first grace, that is, will at least conceive a good thought.[3]

As a concrete way of passing on the knowledge of the rosary, it is recommended that a champion of the rosary seek to give away copies of the following four books on the rosary:

- *The Secret of the Rosary* by St. Louis de Montfort
- *Champions of the Rosary: The History and Heroes of a Spiritual Weapon* by Fr. Donald Calloway, MIC
- *Rosary Gems: Daily Wisdom on the Holy Rosary* by Fr. Donald Calloway, MIC
- *How to Pray the Rosary* by Fr. Donald Calloway, MIC

In addition to evangelizing others by giving them one of the four books above, if your parish does not have a rosary prayer group, try to start one. Always be sure to get the permission of the pastor of the parish first, however. Most times, pastors favor such practices, and will have no problem with people praying the rosary either before or after Mass. Most priests find that this practice fosters a greater sense of devotion in the hearts and souls of their parishioners and leads to a greater participation in the life of the Church.

Other ways to encourage the faithful to pray the rosary, as Bl. Alberione and so many other saints have noted, is to begin to pray it as a family and as spouses. It is also a highly praiseworthy practice for a family to initiate a weekly rosary prayer group in their home and invite other families and parishioners over to pray the rosary. Once this practice catches on, the families and parishioners can begin to alternate homes so that a community of faith is formed and relationships are built. This practice is certain to bring about devout Catholic communities and help build holy families and devout parishes. Whatever way you seek to encourage others to pray the rosary, remember the words of St. Louis de Montfort:

Our Lady blesses not only those who preach her rosary, but she highly rewards all those who get others to say it by their example.[4]

3) Join an official organization that promotes the rosary

Joining an official organization that promotes the rosary is an extraordinary way to champion the rosary and share in the spiritual benefits of the organization. Many of these organizations function as spiritual benefit societies and offer their members many blessings. Organizations such as the Association of Marian Helpers, the Thirteenth of the Month Club, the Legion of Mary, the Schoenstatt Rosary Campaign, the Militia Immaculatae, the World Apostolate of Fatima, and Holy Cross Family Ministries are some of the great organizations that you can join to help spread the rosary.

Two rosary organizations that I particularly recommend are the Thirteenth of the Month Club and the Confraternity of the Rosary. The Thirteenth of the Month Club, based out of Stockbridge, Massachusetts, is operated by the Marian Fathers of the Immaculate Conception, the religious congregation to which I belong. The Marian Fathers operate the National Shrine of The Divine Mercy in Stockbridge and are a zealous group of men promoting devotion to Our Lady (especially as the Immaculate Conception), the Divine Mercy message and devotion, Marian consecration, and the rosary. As the spiritual director for the Thirteenth of the Month Club, I can assure you that it is a very worthwhile group to join, a great way to champion the rosary, and a true means of offering support for a very orthodox Marian religious community. I strongly encourage you to find out more about the Thirteenth of the Month Club and become a member:

Thirteenth of the Month Club
Eden Hill
Stockbridge, MA 01263
1-800-462-7426
www.marian.org/13th

The other rosary organization that I most highly recommend is the Confraternity of the Rosary. This is the worldwide organization that was founded by St. Dominic, renewed by Bl. Alan de la Roche, and has been promoted by many popes. In the United States, contact the Confraternity at either of the following two locations:

Confraternity of the Rosary
PO Box 3617
Portland, OR 97208
1-503-236-8393
www.rosary-center.org

Confraternity of the Rosary
280 North Grant Ave.
Columbus, OH 43215
1-614-240-5929
www.rosaryconfraternity.org

In addition to the above rosary organizations, I also highly recommend that all Catholic men join the Holy League movement, founded in Wisconsin in 2014. This organization has its spiritual headquarters at the Shrine of Our Lady of Guadalupe in La Crosse, Wisconsin; Cardinal Raymond Burke is its spiritual head. The Holy League is a parish-based network of men dedicated to fighting against the evils of our day by means of a monthly Eucharistic Holy Hour, which includes making available the Sacrament of Confession and praying the rosary. It is done in an effort to help Catholic men remain strong in the power of grace.

Holy League
PO Box 1266
La Crosse, WI 54602
www.holyleague.com

WHY PRAY THE ROSARY?

Why pray the rosary? The short answer: *It takes a sword to slay a dragon.* Dear reader, there is a serpent dragon with seven vicious heads who seeks to destroy you (see Rev 12:3). A dragon with one head is threatening enough, but a dragon with seven heads requires a heavenly weapon — the heavenly Queen's weapon. Mary will give you this weapon if you ask for it. Remember the words of Pope Leo XIII:

> The Mother of God, the Virgin most powerful, who in times past co-operated in charity that the faithful might be born in the Church, is now the intermediary, the Mediatrix of our salvation. May she shatter and strike off the multiple heads of the wicked hydra.[1]

There are, of course, many reasons why you should pray the rosary. It would be impossible to list them all. The four most important reasons are listed and explained in the pages that follow.

1) The rosary conquers the evil one

We live in a fallen world where fallen angels (demons) seek to destroy us. Such evil can only be overcome by having a greater weapon than the enemy possesses. Jesus Christ, having bound the dragon, has entrusted to his Church the weapons that enable his followers to be victorious over the evil one. These weapons are the Sacraments and the teachings of the one, holy, catholic, and apostolic Church. It is these mysteries and truths that are encapsulated in the weapon of the rosary.

The rosary is a spiritual sword made by the Divine Craftsman. Popes and saints have repeatedly emphasized this reality. Pope Leo XIII stated very clearly:

> The origin of this form of prayer [the rosary] is divine rather than human.[2]

The genius of this spiritual sword is that it is easily memorized and can be prayed anywhere, anytime, and in almost all circumstances. It encapsulates the life-giving wonders of the Sacraments and the teachings of the Church, and brings them into your home and into every aspect of your life. The rosary is mobile, portable, and greatly feared by the enemy. Saint Louis de Montfort once said:

> The devils have an overwhelming fear of the rosary. Saint Bernard says that the Angelic Salutation puts them to flight and makes all hell tremble.[3]

To pray the rosary is to pray the Word of God. What better devotional prayers could ever be said than the Our Father and the Hail Mary? The words of the Our Father came from the lips of Jesus Christ himself. The words of the Angelic Salutation were uttered on God's behalf by a holy angel (St. Gabriel). God has providentially arranged for the majority of the prayers recited in the rosary to be directed to Mary, because it is through her that the world received the instrument of our salvation, the flesh of the God-Man. Through Mary's cooperation with God, the sacred Flesh and holy mysteries of the God-Man were entrusted to the Church. Through Mary, the God-Man has conquered the darkness and vanquished the evil one forever. This mystery of salvation continues to be worked out in every generation until the end of time. It is especially through the sacred mysteries of the rosary-sword that Jesus continues to win victories over evil through his Mystical Body. Jesus himself said:

> Do not think that I have come to bring peace on earth; I have not come to bring peace, but a sword (Mt 10:34).

The rosary will make you an armed soldier, a sword-wielding knight on the battlefield of life. A rosary a day keeps the devil away!

2) The rosary preaches Jesus Christ and brings peace

The rosary is an evangelical tool that brings the light of Christ into all situations. It has the power to bring about world peace because the mysteries focus on the Truth, that is, on Jesus Christ. The original purpose of the rosary, as revealed to St. Dominic by Our Lady, was to combat heresy (false teachings). This clarification of truth was not just meant for the 13th century, but for all time, since Jesus is the same yesterday, today, and forever (see Heb 13:8). For this reason, Pope Leo XIII rightly stated:

> Our need of divine help is as great today as when the great Dominic introduced the use of the rosary of Mary as a balm for the wounds of his contemporaries.[4]

In subsequent apparitions of Our Lady, such as at Fatima, Mary reiterated that the rosary should be prayed every day in order to help people return to Jesus Christ and have peace. She even noted that the rosary has the power to stop wars. In light of that, it becomes plain that praying the rosary benefits individuals, families, and the entire world. Popes and saints have incessantly taught this reality. Pope Leo XIII emphasized the following in this regard:

> The rosary, if devoutly used, is bound to benefit not only the individual but society at large.[5]

The rosary was born in an age of chivalry. The world is once again in need of knights who are willing to fight for truth and peace. Only truth will bring about world peace. Today's knight must use this spiritual weapon to win people back to the light of the Gospel. The ability of the rosary to change hearts and bring about the reign of Christ has been proven throughout history by causing countless miracles and victories. It has saved marriages, helped turn men into saints, overcome Islam, overthrown dictators, and is one of the most richly indulgenced prayers of the Church. It even has the ability to free souls from purgatory with its indulgences. The forces of darkness in the world today threaten the very foundations of human civilization, but they are no match for the power of the rosary. Historically, the rosary has been proven to overcome all falsehoods. A rosary crusade and a new Holy League are very much needed today to bring the light and peace of Christ back into souls.

3) The rosary teaches virtue

No one ever becomes holy without acquiring virtue. All the virtues that lead to sanctity are exemplified in the lives of Jesus Christ and his Immaculate Mother. The rosary-sword is *the* sacramental that disposes souls to sanctifying grace. It is a proven fact that the rosary draws hearts closer to the Sacraments and the teachings of the Church. By its very nature, the rosary leads a person into a more fervent participation in the life of the Church, especially faithful attendance at Holy Mass and the frequent reception of the Sacrament of Reconciliation (Confession).

In the acquisition of virtue, not only do we have fallen angels and a sinful world to overcome, but we also have the daily struggle to conquer our sinful inclinations and conform our lives to the pattern of all virtue found in Jesus and Mary. Just as children learn how to behave by looking at their parents and imitating them, so the Christian learns to become like Jesus and Mary by meditating on their virtues. The rosary is a tool to prayerfully bring those virtues to mind. Unlike the many New Age practices in the world today that are self-centered and anti-Christian, the rosary offers a form of meditation that leads the soul to true freedom, which can only be found in Jesus Christ. For this reason, the rosary is therapeutic and healing. It helps a person to conquer vice, stop sinning, and acquire virtue. The rosary is heavenly medicine, an antidote that draws the poison of sin and vice out of our hearts.

Perseverance in praying the rosary has proven to be a tremendous means of helping a person avoid sin and remain in a state of grace. Saint Louis de Montfort once wrote:

> It was because Our Lady wanted to help us in the great task of working out our salvation that she ordered St. Dominic to teach the faithful to meditate upon the sacred mysteries of the life of Jesus Christ. She did this, not only that they might adore and glorify him,

but chiefly that they might pattern their lives and actions upon his virtues.[6]

This is one of the many reasons why the rosary is the favored prayer of the saints. The rosary will help you become holy.

4) The rosary is an expression of our love for Jesus and Mary

All people who are in love never tire of telling each other, "I love you." This is also true for parents and their children. Telling someone you love them can have the appearance of a merely repetitious statement, since the same words are repeated over and over again, but everyone knows that telling someone they are loved is never routine or boring. Every time the phrase is uttered, it is new and fresh. The Venerable Fulton Sheen understood this and shared the following insight:

> When we say the rosary — we are saying to God, the Trinity, to the Incarnate Savior, to the Blessed Mother: "I love you, I love you, I love you."[7]

By praying the rosary, we express our gratitude to Jesus and Mary by "calling to mind" the tremendous sacrificial love that they have for us. This act moves the Sacred Heart of Jesus and the Immaculate Heart of Mary to pour out countless graces upon us. Expressions of love from us are reciprocated by gifts of love from heaven.

Saints and popes have often noted in their writings that no one is capable of loving Mary more than Jesus. Therefore, Jesus is not offended when we pray the rosary. On the contrary, he himself takes great delight in the praying of the rosary by his disciples because to pray the rosary is to lay spiritual roses at the feet of his mother. This practice would never offend him. All children would do well to bring flowers to their mother as an expression of love. Would Jesus not inspire others to perform the same loving acts toward his mother that he himself does? After all, he shared the gift of his mother with all of his disciples as he was hanging from the Cross. Thus, when we pray the rosary, we, too, are able to lay lovely garlands of roses at the feet of our beautiful mother. This practice brings joy to the heart of our spiritual mother and greatly pleases the heart of our Savior.

When we pray the rosary, we show that we are faithful to the Word of God, which explicitly states that *all* generations are to call Mary blessed (see Lk 1:48). As Bl. James Alberione succinctly put it:

> The rosary is the easiest way to honor God and the Blessed Virgin. It is the surest way to triumph over spiritual enemies, the most suitable way to progress in virtue and sanctity.[8]

HOW TO PRAY THE ROSARY

The rosary is very easy to pray. It can be prayed on your own or with others. The most important thing to remember about praying the rosary is that it is a blending of vocal and mental (meditative) prayer. Saint Louis de Montfort once remarked:

> I know of no better way of establishing the kingdom
> of God than to unite vocal and mental prayer by saying
> the rosary.[1]

The combination of vocal and mental prayer makes the rosary a prayer of the body and also a prayer of the soul. Having stated this, it is important to remember that if you pray the rosary by yourself, you do not need to vocalize the prayers with your lips.

When praying the rosary, it is better to pray it on one's knees, since this is the most pious position for prayer. Not everyone is able to kneel due to health issues and/or age, and so it is perfectly acceptable to pray the rosary while sitting, walking, exercising, driving, etc. For those who are unfamiliar with the structure of the rosary, a diagram will be presented at the end of this section that includes the prayers associated with the rosary, how it is to be prayed, and a list of the 20 mysteries, as well as which mysteries are prayed on different days of the week. What follows below is a brief description of the vocal and meditative aspects of the rosary.

1) Vocal Prayer

When the rosary is prayed on your own, it should take at least 15 to 20 minutes. It is possible to spend more than 20 minutes praying the rosary and taking more time to meditate on the mysteries. If a person prays the rosary in less than 15 minutes, they are praying it too fast because there really is no way a person can devoutly meditate on the mysteries and say the prayers reverently in less time than that. If a person prays the rosary with other people, the normal amount of time that should be allotted is 20 minutes — no less. There are several dangers to avoid when praying the rosary in a group, including praying the rosary too fast, too slow, too loudly, or emphasizing certain words over others.

Saint Louis de Montfort had the following to say about those who pray the rosary too fast:

> It is really pathetic to see how most people say the holy rosary — they say it astonishingly fast and mumble so that the words are not properly pronounced at all. We could not possibly expect anyone, even the most unimportant person, to think that a slipshod address of this kind was a compliment and yet we expect Jesus and Mary to be pleased with it![2]

These are strong words, but he is absolutely correct. If you have ever tried to pray the rosary with someone who speeds through it, it becomes an endurance test, a burden, and a barely-tolerated act of piety for everyone else. Such a rosary is hardly a meditative prayer at all. As the famous Dominican rosary priest Fr. Gabriel Harty once noted:

> *Speed Kills* is what the road sign shouts. So too with the highway of the rosary. Speed destroys its rhythm and kills the spirit, and the principal victim is the holy name of Jesus.[3]

In other words, when the rosary is prayed in common, everyone should pray it at the same pace, a pace that is not hurried or rushed. Saint Anthony Mary Claret used to instruct his seminarians that when they prayed the rosary, they were to remember that their words were addressed to the King of Kings and the Queen of Heaven and earth. In this regard, he noted the following:

> The rosary should not be prayed hastily, but slowly and with devotion, pronouncing all of the words well, and not starting one part until the other has finished.[4]

Those who pray the rosary in common should also remember that the rosary is not to be prayed too slowly, either. If you have ever prayed the rosary with someone who drags out every word, their voice becomes a distraction and makes the others in attendance feel like they are pushing a heavy train through molasses. When the rosary is prayed too slowly, the other participants cannot meditate because their focus is being drawn to the unnatural pace of the slow person. Forcing others to pray the rosary at that pace is neither charitable nor prayerful for the others in the group.

The rosary is being prayed perfectly when all the members pray it at the same natural and prayerful pace. This gives the rosary a beautiful rhythm, flow, and harmonious timing that match normal breathing patterns. On the other hand, if one member prays too loudly, allowing his voice and pace to dominate the others, everyone automatically begins to focus on his voice and is no longer able to meditate; the vocal aspect becomes a distraction for all the other members. Similarly, if a person places an emphasis on one particular word of the Hail Mary prayer, it breaks the flow and rhythm of the group's timing. All of the above aspects should be taken seriously, because a group's failure to pray the rosary well and harmoniously is often the reason why many people do not join in praying the rosary before or after Mass. Very few people are interested in praying a rosary that is chaotic and a verbal wrestling match. If you desire to hear a perfectly timed and well-prayed communal rosary, visit any chapel of the Missionaries of Charity and listen to how they pray the rosary in common.

2) Meditative Prayer

It is true that most people become easily distracted when praying the rosary. Almost everyone will find their mind wandering away from the mysteries at least once. Even saints struggled with this. God is well aware that we are neither angels nor robots, and do not have the ability to ponder one thing for long periods of time without other things coming to mind. Saint Thérèse of Lisieux expressed her struggles this way:

> I feel that I say the rosary so poorly! I make a concentrated effort to meditate on the mysteries of the rosary, but I am unable to focus my concentration. For a long

time I was disconsolate about my lack of devotion, which astonished me since I so much loved the Blessed Virgin that it ought to have been easy for me to recite the prayers in her honor that so much pleased her. But now I am less sad, for I think that the Queen of heaven, who is also my Mother, ought to see my good intentions and that she is pleased with them.[5]

Everyone who prays the rosary is going to lose their concentration and find their mind wandering from time to time. Do not let this discourage you. Praying the rosary is an act of the will because it is an act of love. Feelings will come and go. True love perseveres through difficulties, distractions, and no sensible consolation. When distractions come, simply re-focus your mind on the mystery at hand. This may occur many times throughout the rosary, but it is very pleasing to Jesus and Mary when a person turns their mind and heart back to the mysteries. Saint Louis de Montfort noted the following in this regard:

Even if you have to fight distractions all through your whole rosary, be sure to fight well, arms in hand: that is to say, do not stop saying your rosary even if it is hard to say and you have absolutely no sensible devotion. It is a terrible battle, I know, but one that is profitable to the faithful soul.[6]

A person will learn many virtues by perseverance in praying the rosary and, over time, will acquire the ability to become less distracted and more focused on the mysteries. The Servant of God Dolindo Ruotolo offers these consoling and encouraging words for those who struggle in this area:

To know how to pray is a gift of God. It is part of the gift of piety, a gift of the Holy Spirit. With diligent practice every day, it is possible to succeed in reciting the holy rosary worthily.[7]

Perseverance makes a champion!

Praying the Rosary

1. Make the Sign of the Cross and say the "Apostles' Creed."

2. Say the "Our Father."

3. Say three "Hail Marys."

4. Say the "Glory be to the Father."

5. Announce the First Mystery; then say the "Our Father."

6. Say 10 "Hail Marys" while meditating on the Mystery.

7. Say the "Glory be to the Father." After each decade, say the following prayer requested

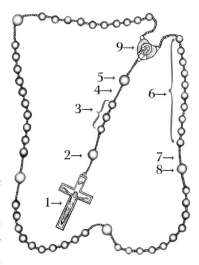

by the Blessed Virgin Mary at Fatima: "O my Jesus, forgive us our sins, save us from the fires of hell, lead all souls to Heaven, especially those in most need of Thy mercy."

8. Announce the Second Mystery: then say the "Our Father." Repeat 6 and 7 and continue with the Third, Fourth, and Fifth Mysteries in the same manner.

9. Say the "Hail, Holy Queen" and the concluding prayer on the medal after the five decades are completed.

As a general rule, depending on the liturgical season, the various Mysteries of the rosary are prayed on the following days of the week:

SUNDAY:	Glorious Mysteries
MONDAY:	Joyful Mysteries
TUESDAY:	Sorrowful Mysteries
WEDNESDAY:	Glorious Mysteries
THURSDAY:	Luminous Mysteries
FRIDAY:	Sorrowful Mysteries
SATURDAY:	Joyful Mysteries

Prayers of the Rosary

THE SIGN OF THE CROSS

In the name of the Father, and of the Son, and of the Holy Spirit. Amen.

THE APOSTLES' CREED

I believe in God, the Father almighty, Creator of heaven and earth, and in Jesus Christ, his only Son, our Lord, who was conceived by the Holy Spirit, born of the Virgin Mary, suffered under Pontius Pilate, was crucified, died, and was buried; he descended into hell; on the third day he rose again from the dead; he ascended into heaven, and is seated at the right hand of God the Father almighty; from there he will come to judge the living and the dead. I believe in the Holy Spirit, the holy catholic Church, the communion of saints, the forgiveness of sins, the resurrection of the body, and life everlasting. Amen.

The wording of the Apostles' Creed conforms with the Roman Missal.

OUR FATHER

Our Father, who art in heaven; hallowed be Thy name; Thy kingdom come; Thy will be done on earth as it is in heaven. Give us this day our daily bread; and forgive us our trespasses as we forgive those who trespass against us, and lead us not into temptation; but deliver us from evil. Amen.

HAIL MARY

Hail Mary, full of grace. The Lord is with thee. Blessed art thou among women, and blessed is the fruit of thy womb, Jesus. Holy Mary, Mother of God, pray for us sinners, now and at the hour of our death. Amen.

GLORY BE TO THE FATHER

Glory be to the Father, and to the Son, and to the Holy Spirit. As it was in the beginning, is now, and ever shall be, world without end. Amen.

FATIMA PRAYER

O my Jesus, forgive us our sins, save us from the fires of hell. Lead all souls to Heaven, especially those most in need of Thy mercy.

HAIL, HOLY QUEEN

Hail, Holy Queen, Mother of Mercy, our life, our sweetness, and our hope, to thee do we cry, poor banished children of Eve; to thee do we send up our sighs, mourning and weeping in this valley of tears; turn, then, most gracious Advocate, thine eyes of mercy towards us, and after this, our exile, show unto us the blessed fruit of thy womb, Jesus. O clement, O loving, O sweet Virgin Mary!

Pray for us, O holy Mother of God, that we may be made worthy of the promises of Christ.

CONCLUDING PRAYER

O God, whose only begotten Son, by His life, death, and resurrection, has purchased for us the rewards of eternal life, grant, we beseech Thee, that by meditating on these mysteries of the most holy Rosary of the Blessed Virgin Mary, we may imitate what they contain and obtain what they promise, through the same Christ our Lord. Amen.

Queen of the Rosary and St. Dominic by Vivian Imbruglia. (2016). Commissioned by Fr. Donald H. Calloway, MIC. www.sacredimageicons.com

Mysteries of the Rosary

JOYFUL MYSTERIES

FIRST JOYFUL MYSTERY

THE ANNUNCIATION

And when the angel had come to her, he said, "Hail, full of grace, the Lord is with you" (Lk 1:28).

One Our Father, 10 Hail Marys, One Glory Be, etc.

FRUIT OF THE MYSTERY: *HUMILITY*

SECOND JOYFUL MYSTERY

THE VISITATION

Elizabeth, filled with the holy Spirit, cried out in a loud voice and said, "Most blessed are you among women, and blessed is the fruit of your womb" (Lk 1:41-42).

One Our Father, 10 Hail Marys, One Glory Be, etc.

FRUIT OF THE MYSTERY: *LOVE OF NEIGHBOR*

THIRD JOYFUL MYSTERY

THE BIRTH OF JESUS

She gave birth to her firstborn Son. She wrapped Him in swaddling clothes and laid Him in a manger, because there was no room for them in the inn (Lk 2:7).

One Our Father, 10 Hail Marys, One Glory Be, etc.

FRUIT OF THE MYSTERY: *POVERTY IN SPIRIT*

FOURTH JOYFUL MYSTERY
THE PRESENTATION

When the days were completed for their purification according to the law of Moses, they took Him up to Jerusalem to present Him to the Lord, just as it is written in the law of the Lord, "Every male that opens the womb shall be consecrated to the Lord" (Lk 2:22-23).

One Our Father, 10 Hail Marys, One Glory Be, etc.

FRUIT OF THE MYSTERY:
OBEDIENCE

FIFTH JOYFUL MYSTERY
FINDING THE CHILD JESUS IN THE TEMPLE

After three days they found Him in the temple, sitting in the midst of the teachers, listening to them and asking them questions (Lk 2:46).

One Our Father, 10 Hail Marys, One Glory Be, etc.

FRUIT OF THE MYSTERY:
JOY IN FINDING JESUS

LUMINOUS MYSTERIES

FIRST LUMINOUS MYSTERY
BAPTISM OF JESUS

After Jesus was baptized, ... the heavens were opened [for Him], and he saw the Spirit of God descending like a dove [and] coming upon Him. And a voice came from the heavens, saying, "This is My beloved Son, with whom I am well pleased" (Mt 3:16-17).

One Our Father, 10 Hail Marys, One Glory Be, etc.

FRUIT OF THE MYSTERY:
OPENNESS TO THE HOLY SPIRIT

SECOND LUMINOUS MYSTERY
WEDDING AT CANA

His mother said to the servers, "Do whatever He tells you." ... Jesus told them, "Fill the jars with water." So they filled them to the brim (Jn 2:5-7).

One Our Father, 10 Hail Marys, One Glory Be, etc.

FRUIT OF THE MYSTERY:
TO JESUS THROUGH MARY

THIRD LUMINOUS MYSTERY
PROCLAIMING THE KINGDOM

"As you go, make this proclamation: 'The kingdom of heaven is at hand.' Cure the sick, raise the dead, cleanse lepers, drive out demons. Without cost you have received; without cost you are to give" (Mt 10:7-8).

One Our Father, 10 Hail Marys, One Glory Be, etc.

FRUIT OF THE MYSTERY:
REPENTANCE AND TRUST IN GOD

FOURTH LUMINOUS MYSTERY
TRANSFIGURATION

While He was praying His face changed in appearance and His clothing became dazzling white. Then from the cloud came a voice that said, "This is My chosen Son; listen to Him" (Lk 9:29, 35).

One Our Father, 10 Hail Marys, One Glory Be, etc.

FRUIT OF THE MYSTERY:
DESIRE FOR HOLINESS

FIFTH LUMINOUS MYSTERY
INSTITUTION OF THE EUCHARIST

Then He took the bread, said the blessing, broke it, and gave it to them, saying, "This is My body, which will be given for you ..." And likewise the cup after they had eaten, saying, "This cup is the new covenant in My blood" (Lk 22:19-20).

One Our Father, 10 Hail Marys, One Glory Be, etc.

FRUIT OF THE MYSTERY: *ADORATION*

SORROWFUL MYSTERIES

FIRST SORROWFUL MYSTERY
THE AGONY IN THE GARDEN

He was in such agony and He prayed so fervently that His sweat became like drops of blood falling on the ground. When He rose from prayer and returned to His disciples, He found them sleeping from grief (Lk 22:44-45).

One Our Father, 10 Hail Marys, One Glory Be, etc.

FRUIT OF THE MYSTERY: *SORROW FOR SIN*

SECOND SORROWFUL MYSTERY
THE SCOURGING AT THE PILLAR

Then Pilate took Jesus and had Him scourged (Jn 19:1).

One Our Father, 10 Hail Marys, One Glory Be, etc.

FRUIT OF THE MYSTERY: *PURITY*

THIRD SORROWFUL MYSTERY

CROWNING WITH THORNS

They stripped off His clothes and threw a scarlet military cloak about Him. Weaving a crown out of thorns, they placed it on His head, and a reed in His right hand (Mt 27:28-29).

One Our Father, 10 Hail Marys, One Glory Be, etc.

FRUIT OF THE MYSTERY: *COURAGE*

FOURTH SORROWFUL MYSTERY

CARRYING OF THE CROSS

And carrying the cross Himself, He went out to what is called the Place of the Skull, in Hebrew, Golgotha (Jn 19:17).

One Our Father, 10 Hail Marys, One Glory Be, etc.

FRUIT OF THE MYSTERY: *PATIENCE*

FIFTH SORROWFUL MYSTERY

THE CRUCIFIXION

Jesus cried out in a loud voice, "Father, into Your hands I commend My spirit"; and when He had said this He breathed His last (Lk 23:46).

One Our Father, 10 Hail Marys, One Glory Be, etc.

FRUIT OF THE MYSTERY: *PERSEVERANCE*

GLORIOUS MYSTERIES

FIRST GLORIOUS MYSTERY
THE RESURRECTION

"Do not be amazed! You seek Jesus of Nazareth, the crucified. He has been raised; He is not here. Behold the place where they laid Him" (Mk16:6).

One Our Father, 10 Hail Marys, One Glory Be, etc.

FRUIT OF THE MYSTERY:
FAITH

SECOND GLORIOUS MYSTERY
THE ASCENSION

So then the Lord Jesus, after He spoke to them, was taken up into heaven and took His seat at the right hand of God (Mk 16:19).

One Our Father, 10 Hail Marys, One Glory Be, etc.

FRUIT OF THE MYSTERY:
HOPE

THIRD GLORIOUS MYSTERY
DESCENT OF THE HOLY SPIRIT

And they were all filled with the Holy Spirit and began to speak in different tongues, as the Spirit enabled them to proclaim (Acts 2:4).

One Our Father, 10 Hail Marys, One Glory Be, etc.

FRUIT OF THE MYSTERY:
LOVE OF GOD

FOURTH GLORIOUS MYSTERY

THE ASSUMPTION

"You are the glory of Jerusalem! ... You are the great boast of our nation! ... You have done good things for Israel, and God is pleased with them. May the Almighty Lord bless you forever!" (Jud 15:9-10).

One Our Father, 10 Hail Marys, One Glory Be, etc.

FRUIT OF THE MYSTERY: *GRACE OF A HAPPY DEATH*

FIFTH GLORIOUS MYSTERY

THE CORONATION

A great sign appeared in the sky, a woman clothed with the sun, with the moon under her feet, and on her head a crown of twelve stars (Rev 12:1).

One Our Father, 10 Hail Marys, One Glory Be, etc.

FRUIT OF THE MYSTERY: *TRUST IN MARY'S INTERCESSION*

THE 15 PROMISES OF OUR LADY TO THOSE WHO PRAY THE ROSARY

1) To all those who shall recite my rosary devoutly, I promise my special protection and very great graces.

2) Those who shall persevere in the recitation of my rosary shall receive signal graces.

3) The rosary shall be a very powerful armor against hell; it will destroy vice, deliver from sin, and dispel heresy.

4) The rosary will make virtue and good works flourish, and will obtain for souls the most abundant divine mercies; it will draw the hearts of men from the love of the world to the love of God, and will lift them to the desire of eternal things. How many souls shall sanctify themselves by this means!

5) Those who trust themselves to me through the rosary shall not perish.

6) Those who shall recite my rosary devoutly, meditating on its mysteries, shall not be overwhelmed by misfortune. The sinner shall be converted; the just shall grow in grace and become worthy of eternal life.

7) Those truly devoted to my rosary shall not die without the Sacraments of the Church.

8) Those who faithfully recite my rosary shall find during their life and at the hour of their death the light of God, the fullness of his graces, and shall share in the merits of the blessed.

9) I shall deliver very promptly from purgatory the souls devoted to my rosary.

10) The true children of my rosary shall enjoy great glory in heaven.

11) What you ask through my rosary, you shall obtain.

12) Those who propagate my rosary will be aided by me in all their necessities.

13) I have obtained from my Son that all the members of the Rosary Confraternity shall have as their intercessors, in life and in death, the entire celestial court.

14) Those who recite my rosary faithfully are all my beloved children, the brothers and sisters of Jesus Christ.

15) Devotion to my rosary is a great sign of predestination.

* The above list is taken from a book by the Servant of God Patrick Peyton.[1]

St. Dominic: Champion of the Holy Rosary by Nellie Edwards. (2016). Commissioned by Fr. Donald H. Calloway, MIC. www.PaintedFaith.net

INDULGENCES
OF THE ROSARY

P eople are often quite unaware of how rich the rosary is in indulgences. This is because many priests, when preaching on the rosary, hardly ever mention indulgences and give rather a flowery and popular sermon which excites admiration but scarcely teaches anything.[1]

~ St. Louis de Montfort

The words above serve as a reminder that, over the course of the centuries, there have been many indulgences given by the Church to those who pray the rosary. The Catholic Church is the storehouse of the graces of the redemption, and the Savior works through his Mystical Body to dispense many of these graces to souls in the form of pardons. These gifts are not magic, but rather graces and mercies that flow from the heart of a merciful God who loves his children. Our Heavenly Father is more than willing to indulge us with his mercy and love.

On January 1, 1967, Bl. Pope Paul VI promulgated a revision of the sacred indulgences available to the Church in an apostolic constitution titled *Indulgentiarum Doctrina*. It was published on June 29, 1968 and has since undergone several editions. On July 5, 1999, in preparation for the Jubilee celebrations for the third Christian millennium, St. John Paul II approved a revised fourth edition. Then, on October 12, 2005, the Apostolic Penitentiary in Rome approved the English translation of the text, now known in English as the *Manual of Indulgences*.

Below are the selected and pertinent *Norms* from the *Manual of Indulgences* that the reader will find helpful for understanding what an indulgence is (plenary or partial), how often one may be obtained, and what conditions must be met to gain it. Presented at the end are the specific indulgenced Grants from the *Manual of Indulgences* that the Church offers to those who pray the rosary.

NORMS

n. 1 — An indulgence is a remission before God of the temporal punishment for sins, whose guilt is forgiven, which a properly disposed member of the Christian faithful obtains under certain and clearly defined conditions through the intervention of the Church, which, as the minister of Redemption, dispenses and applies authoritatively the treasury of the expiatory works of Christ and the saints.

n. 2 — An indulgence is partial or plenary according to whether it removes either part or all of the temporal punishment due sin.

n. 3 — The faithful can obtain partial or plenary indulgences for themselves, or they can apply them to the dead [souls in purgatory] by way of suffrage. [No one gaining an indulgence may apply it to other living persons.]

n. 15 — The faithful can acquire an indulgence if they use devoutly one of the following properly blessed pious objects, namely, a crucifix or cross, rosary, scapular, or medal.

n. 17 — In order to be capable of gaining indulgences one must be baptized, not excommunicated, and in the state of grace at least at the completion of the prescribed works.

n. 18 — A plenary indulgence can be acquired only once in the course of a day; a partial indulgence can be acquired multiple times.

n. 20 — To gain a plenary indulgence, in addition to excluding all attachment to sin, even venial sin, it is necessary to perform the indulgenced work and fulfill the following three conditions: sacramental confession, Eucharistic Communion, and prayer for the intention of the Sovereign Pontiff.

- The three conditions may be fulfilled several days before or after the performance of the prescribed work; it is, however fitting that Communion be received and the prayer for the intention of the Holy Father be said on the same day the work is performed.

- The condition of praying for the intention of the Holy Father is fully satisfied by reciting one Our Father and one

Hail Mary; nevertheless, one has the option of reciting any other prayer according to individual piety and devotion, if recited for this intention.

* Many numbers have not been presented because they are not pertinent to the topic at hand.

GRANTS

n. 17 — Prayers to the Blessed Virgin Mary

A plenary indulgence is granted to the faithful who

• devoutly recite the Marian rosary in a church or oratory, or in a family, a religious community, or an association of the faithful, and in general when several of the faithful gather for some honest purpose;

• devoutly join in the recitation of the rosary while it is being recited by the Supreme Pontiff and broadcast live by radio or television. In other circumstances, the indulgence will be *partial*.

NB: According to the *Manual of Indulgences*, the plenary indulgence is gained when only five decades of the rosary are recited. However, the five decades must be recited without interruption.[2]

References

CHAMPIONS OF THE ROSARY

* *Initial quote:*
~ St. Faustina Kowalska, *Diary: Divine Mercy in My Soul,* third edition (Stockbridge, MA: Marian Press, 2002), entry 450.

(The references listed below are in the same order in which they appear for each Champion)

St. Dominic

* Image on pg. 13: *The Virgin Presenting the Rosary to St. Dominic* by Antonio Palomino (1655-1726). Seattle Art Museum. Used with permission.

~ *"Our Lady's words to St. Dominic,"* as quoted in Augusta Theodosia Drane, OP, *The History of St. Dominic: Founder of the Friars Preachers* (London: Longmans, Green, and Co., 1891), 122.

~ Pope Alexander VI, as quoted in William G. Most, *Mary in Our Life* (Garden City, NY: Image Books, 1963), 305.

~ St. Pope Pius V, *Consueverunt Romani Pontifices,* Papal Bull *(September 17, 1569).*

~ Servant of God Pope Benedict XIII, as quoted in William G. Most, *Mary in Our Life.* (Garden City, NY: Image Books, 1963), 306.

~ St. Louis de Montfort, *The Secret of the Rosary,* trans. Mary Barbour, TOP, (Bay Shore, NY: Montfort Publications, 1988), 18.

~ Ibid., 22.

~ Ibid., 27.

~ Ibid., 69.

~ Ibid., 74.

~ Ibid., 101.

~ Bl. Pope Pius IX, as quoted in Deacon Andrew J. Gerakas, *The Rosary and Devotion to Mary* (Boston, MA: St. Paul Books & Media, 1992), 20.

~ Bl. John Henry Newman, *Sayings of Cardinal Newman* (Dublin: Carraig Books, 1976), 44-46.

~ Pope Leo XIII, *Adiutricem,* Encyclical (September 5, 1895), 12.

~ Pope Leo XIII, *Supremi Apostolatus Officio,* 3.

~ Ibid., 8.

~ Pope Leo XIII, as quoted in Robert Feeney, *The Rosary: "The Little Summa,"* fourth edition (USA: Aquinas Press, 2003), 10.

~ Pope Benedict XV, *Fausto Appetente Die,* Encyclical (June 29, 1921), 11.

~ Servant of God Joseph Kentenich, as quoted in Fr. Jonathan Niehaus, *New Vision and Life: The Founding of Schoenstatt (1912-1919)* (Waukesha, WI: Schoenstatt Fathers, 2004), 32.

~ Bl. James Alberione, *Mary, Mother and Model: Feasts of Mary,* trans. Hilda Calabro, MA (Boston, MA: Daughters of St. Paul, 1958), 202.

~ Bl. James Alberione, *Lord, Teach Us to Pray* (Boston, MA: Daughters of St. Paul, 1982), 223.

~ Ibid., 225.

~ Ven. Fulton J. Sheen, *The World's First Love: Mary, Mother of God* (San Francisco: Ignatius Press, 1996), 206.

~ Servant of God Patrick J. Peyton, *The Ear of God* (Garden City, NY: Doubleday & Company, Inc., 1951), 113.

~ Pope Benedict XVI, *Angelus message* (October 7, 2007).

Recommended Reading on St. Dominic

~ St. Louis de Montfort, *The Secret of the Rosary,* trans. Mary Barbour, TOP (Bay Shore, NY: Montfort Publications, 1988).

~ Pope Benedict XV, *Fausto Appetente Die* (Encyclical Letter on St. Dominic). June 29, 1921.

~ J.M.P. Heaney, OP, *A Short Treatise on the Rosary* (New York: Dominicans, 1863).

~ Augusta Theodosia Drane, OP, *The History of St. Dominic: Founder of the Friars Preachers* (London: Longmans, Green, and Co., 1891).

~ John Procter, OP, *The Rosary Guide for Priests and People* (London: Kegan and Trubner, 1901).

~ Wilfrid Lescher, OP, *St. Dominic and the Rosary* (London: R. & T. Washbourne, 1902).

~ Andrew Skelly, OP, *St. Dominic and the Rosary.* (Providence, RI: Providence College Digital Commons), *Historical Catholic and Dominican Documents. Book 1,* (1915).

~ Humbert Clerissac, OP, *The Spirit of St. Dominic* (Mercer Island, WA: Cluny Media LLC, 2015). Reprinted from the 1939 edition.

Blessed Alan de la Roche

* Image on pg. 22: Berlin/Kupferstichkabinett, Staatliche Museen, Berlin, Germany/Herbert Boswank/Art Resource, NY. Used with permission.

~ Bl. Alan de la Roche, as quoted in Rev. Charles G. Fehrenbach,

CSsR, *Mary Day by Day* (New York: Catholic Book Publishing Co., 1987), 147.

~ Bl. Alan de la Roche, as quoted in St. Louis de Montfort, *The Secret of the Rosary,* trans. Mary Barbour, TOP (Bay Shore, NY: Montfort Publications, 1988), 21.

~ St. Louis de Montfort, *The Secret of the Rosary,* trans. Mary Barbour, TOP (Bay Shore, NY: Montfort Publications, 1988), 23.

~ Ibid., 23.

~ Ibid., 23-24.

~ Ibid., 84.

~ Ibid., 86.

~ Ibid., 68-69.

~ Ibid., 66.

~ Ibid., 67.

~ Ibid., 81.

~ St. Alphonsus Liguori, as quoted in Susan Tassone, *Day By Day for the Holy Souls in Purgatory: 365 Reflections* (Huntington, IN: Our Sunday Visitor, Inc., 2014), 298.

~ Bl. James Alberione, *Lest We Forget* (Boston, MA: Daughters of St. Paul, 1967), 143.

~ Bl. Gabriele Allegra, *Mary's Immaculate Heart: A Way to God* (Chicago, IL: Franciscan Herald Press, 1985), 72.

Recommended Reading on Bl. Alan de la Roche

~ St. Louis de Montfort, *The Secret of the Rosary,* trans. Mary Barbour, TOP (Bay Shore, NY: Montfort Publications, 1988).

~ Dominican Fathers, "The Life and Times of B. Alain de la Roche in the Fifteenth Century: Restorer of the Confraternity of the Most Holy Rosary," in *The Monthly Magazine of the Holy Rosary,* no. 1 (August, 1872), 13-16; no. 2 (September, 1872), 32-35.

~ Raymond P. Devas, OP, "The Rosary Tradition Defined and Defended," in *American Catholic Quarterly Review,* vol. XLI (January, 1916), 128-147.

~ William G. Most, *Mary in Our Life* (Garden City, NY: Image Books, 1963).

~ John S. Johnson, *The Rosary in Action* (Charlotte, NC: TAN Books, 1977).

~ Michael Müller, CSsR, *The Devotion of the Holy Rosary* (Fitzwilliam, NH: Loreto Publications, 2011).

~ Pepin Guglielmo, OP, *Il Salutate Mariam* (Firenze, Italia: 1950).

St. Pope Pius V

~ St. Pope Pius V, *Consueverunt Romani Pontifices,* Papal Bull (September 17, 1569).

~ Ibid.

~ St. Pope Pius V, as quoted in Deacon Andrew J. Gerakas, *The Rosary and Devotion to Mary* (Boston, MA: St. Paul Books & Media, 1992), 21.

~ St. Pope Pius V, as quoted in David Supple, *Virgin Wholly Marvelous* (Cambridge, MA: Ravengate, 1991), 131.

~ St. Pope Pius V, as quoted in Wilfrid Lescher, OP, *St. Dominic and the Rosary* (London: R. & T. Washbourne, 1902), 11.

~ St. Louis de Montfort, *The Secret of the Rosary,* trans. Mary Barbour, TOP (Bay Shore, NY: Montfort Publications, 1988), 64-65.

~ Pope Benedict XV, *Fausto Appetente Die,* Encyclical (June 29, 1921), 11.

~ Servant of God Joseph Kentenich, as quoted in Fr. Jonathan Neihaus, *New Vision and Life: The Founding of Schoenstatt (1912-1919)* (Waukesha, WI: Schoenstatt Fathers, 2004), 35.

Recommended Reading on St. Pope Pius V

~ St. Pope Pius V, *Consueverunt Romani Pontifices* (September 17, 1569).

~ St. Pope Pius V, *Salvatoris Domini* (March 5, 1571).

~ Catherine M. Antony, *Saint Pius V: Pope of the Holy Rosary* (London: Longmans, Green and Co., 1911).

~ G.K. Chesterton, *Lepanto* (San Francisco, CA: Ignatius Press, 2003).

~ Robin Anderson, *St. Pius V: His Life, Times and Miracles* (Charlotte, NC: TAN Books, 2009).

St. Louis de Montfort

* Image on pg. 34: O.D.M. pinxit, Editions Magnificat, Mont-Tremblant, Québec. Used with permission.

~ St. Louis de Montfort, *God Alone: The Collected Writings of St. Louis de Montfort* (Bay Shore, NY: Montfort Publications, 1995), 421.

~ St. Louis de Montfort, *The Secret of the Rosary,* trans. Mary Barbour, TOP (Bay Shore, NY: Montfort Publications, 1988), 27.

~ Ibid., 9.

~ Ibid., 9.

~ Ibid., 16.

~ Ibid., 9.

~ Ibid., 17-18.

~ Ibid., 98.

~ Ibid., 26.

~ Ibid., 27.

~ Ibid., 29.

~ Ibid., 85.

~ Ibid., 62.

~ Ibid., 67.

~ Ibid., 71.

~ Ibid., 13.

~ Ibid., 97.

~ Ibid., 98.

~ Ibid., 12.

~ St. Louis de Montfort, as quoted in Rev. Charles G. Fehrenbach, CSsR, *Mary Day by Day* (New York: Catholic Book Publishing Co., 1987), 149.

~ St. Louis de Montfort, *God Alone: The Collected Writings of St. Louis de Montfort,* 403.

Recommended Reading on St. Louis de Montfort

~ St. Louis de Montfort, *The Secret of the Rosary,* trans. Mary Barbour, TOP (Bay Shore, NY: Montfort Publications, 1954).

~ St. Louis de Montfort, *True Devotion to the Blessed Virgin* (Bay Shore, NY: Montfort Publications, 1996).

~ St. Louis de Montfort, *God Alone: The Collected Writings of St. Louis de Montfort* (Bay Shore, NY: Montfort Publications, 1995).

~ St. Louis de Montfort, *Jesus Living in Mary: Handbook on the Spirituality of St. Louis Marie de Montfort* (Bay Shore, NY: Montfort Publications, 1995).

St. Alphonsus Liguori

* Image on pg. 41: Courtesy of the Redemptorists. Used with permission.

~ St. Alphonsus Liguori, *Hail Holy Queen: An Explanation of the Salve Regina.* (Charlotte, NC: TAN Books, 1995), 225-226.

~ Ibid., 226.

~ Ibid., 226.

~ Ibid., 226.

~ St. Alphonsus Liguori, *The Glories of Mary* (Charlotte, NC: TAN Books, 2012), 545. Used with permission.

~ Ibid., 546.

~ Ibid., 546.

~ Ibid., 545.

~ St. Alphonsus Liguori, *The Glories of Mary* (Brooklyn, NY: Redemptorist Fathers, 1931), 599.

~ St. Alphonsus Liguori, as quoted in Catherine Moran, *Praying the Rosary with the Saints* [E-reader version], 2013.

~ St. Alphonsus Liguori, *Hail Holy Queen: An Explanation of the Salve Regina*, 226.

Recommended Reading on St. Alphonsus Liguori

~ St. Alphonsus Liguori, *Hail Holy Queen: An Explanation of the Salve Regina* (Charlotte, NC: TAN Books, 1995).

~ St. Alphonsus Liguori, *The Glories of Mary* (Charlotte, NC: TAN Books, 2012).

~ Fr. Donald H. Calloway, MIC, *Marian Gems: Daily Wisdom on Our Lady* (Stockbridge, MA: Marian Press, 2014).

~ Fr. Donald H. Calloway, MIC, *Rosary Gems: Daily Wisdom on the Holy Rosary* (Stockbridge, MA: Marian Press, 2015).

Blessed Pope Pius IX

~ Bl. Pope Pius IX, as quoted in *The Official Handbook of the Legion of Mary* (Dublin: Concilium Legionis Mariae, 2005), 146.

~ Bl. Pope Pius IX, as quoted in Msgr. Joseph A. Cirrincione and Thomas A. Nelson, *The Rosary and the Crisis of Faith* (Charlotte, NC: TAN Books, 1986), 35.

~ Bl. Pope Pius IX, as quoted in Don Sharkey, *The Woman Shall Conquer: The Story of the Blessed Virgin in the Modern World* (Milwaukee: Bruce Publishing Company, 1952), 246.

~ Bl. Pope Pius IX, as quoted in Patrick J. Peyton, *The Ear of God* (Garden City, NY: Doubleday, 1951), 107.

~ Bl. Pope Pius IX, as quoted in Wilfrid Lescher, OP, *St. Dominic and the Rosary.* (London: R. & T. Washbourne, 1902), 8.

~ Ibid., 8-9.

~ Bl. Pope Pius IX, as quoted in M. Josef Frings, *The Excellence of the Rosary: Conferences for Devotions in Honor of the Blessed Virgin* (New York: Wagner, 1912), 9.

~ Bl. Pope Pius IX, as quoted in Wilfrid Lescher, OP, *St. Dominic and the Rosary,* 8-9.

~ Bl. Pope Pius IX, *Ad Perpetuam rei memorium (Papal Bull grant-ing indulgences to the Members of the Association of the Perpetual Rosary,* April 12, 1868), quoted in *The Monthly Magazine of the Rosary* (December, 1872), 130-131.

~ Bl. Pope Pius IX, as quoted in *Rosary* (Revised edition of the spe-cial rosary issue of *The Immaculate* magazine, 1970), 40. Originally published in vol. 16. no. 5 (October 1965).

Recommended Reading on Bl. Pope Pius IX

~ Bl. Pope Pius IX, *Eregus Sues,* Apostolic Letter (December 3, 1869).

~ Bl. Pope Pius IX, *C'est un Fait Eclant. To the Superior and Missonaries of the Sanctuary of Lourdes,* Apostolic Letter (February 8, 1875).

~ Bl. Pope Pius IX, *Ubi Primum,* Encyclical (February 2, 1849).

~ Bl. Pope Pius IX, *Ineffabilis Deus,* Apostolic Constitution (Decem-ber 8, 1854).

~ Fr. Donald H. Calloway, MIC, ed., *The Immaculate Conception in the Life of the Church* (Stockbridge, MA: Marian Press, 2004).

St. Anthony Mary Claret

* Image on pg. 51: General Government, Claretian Missionaries, Rome, Italy. Used with permission

~ St. Anthony Mary Claret, *Autobiography.* ed., Jose Maria Vinas, CMF (Chicago, IL: Claretian Publications, 1976), 14-15.

~ Ibid., 38.

~ Ibid., 38.

~ Ibid., 17.

~ Ibid., 237.

~ St. Anthony Mary Claret, as quoted in Fr. Juan Echevarria, *The Miracles of St. Anthony Mary Claret,* trans. Sr. Mary Gonzaga (Char-lotte, NC: TAN Books, 1992), 61.

~ St. Anthony Mary Claret, *El Colegial Ó Seminarista Teórica y Prác-ticamente Instruido: Tome II* (Barcelona, Spain: Librería Religiosa, 1861), 503. Trans. Miss Ileana E. Salazar, MA.

~ St. Anthony Mary Claret, *The Golden Key to Heaven* (Buffalo, NY: Immaculate Heart Publications, 1955), 358.

~ St. Anthony Mary Claret, *El Colegial Ó Seminarista Teórica y Prác-ticamente Instruido: Tome II* (Barcelona, Spain: Librería Religiosa, 1861), 503. Trans. Miss Ileana E. Salazar, MA.

~ St. Anthony Mary Claret, *Autobiography,* 241.

~ Ibid., 115.

~ St. Anthony Mary Claret, as quoted in Juan Maria Lozano, CMF, *Mystic and Man of Action: Saint Anthony Mary Claret,* trans. Joseph Daries, CMF (Chicago, IL: Claretian Publications, 1977), 141.

~ St. Anthony Mary Claret, *El Colegial Ó Seminarista Teórica y Prácticamente Instruido: Tome I.* (Barcelona, Spain: Librería Religiosa, 1861), 276. Trans. Miss Ileana E. Salazar, MA.

~ Ibid., 276.

~ Ibid., 277.

~ Ibid., 277.

~ Ibid., 277.

~ Ibid., 277.

~ Ibid., 277.

~ Ibid., 341.

~ Ibid., 279.

~ St. Anthony Mary Claret, *Autobiography,* 95.

Recommended Reading on St. Anthony Mary Claret

~ St. Anthony Mary Claret, *Autobiography.* (ed.) Jose Maria Vinas, CMF (Chicago, IL: Claretian Publications, 1976).

~ St. Anthony Mary Claret, *Devocion del Santísimo Rosario* (Barcelona, Spain: Libreria Religiosa, 1858).

~ St. Anthony Mary Claret, *El Santísimo Rosario Explicado* (Barcelona, Spain: Libreria Religiosa, 1864).

~ Gabriel Mary Mesina, FI, "Saint Anthony Mary Claret: Son of the Immaculate Heart of Mary," in *Missio Immaculatae,* vol. 11. no.1 (January/February, 2015), 17-23.

~ Juan Echevarria, *The Miracles of St. Anthony Mary Claret,* trans. Sr. Mary Gonzaga (Charlotte, NC: TAN Books, 1992).

~ Perrin, Joseph-Marie, "Le V Antoine-Marie Claret, archeveque. Le Dominique de xix siècle." *Revue de Rosaire* 10 (1931): 296-302, 329-337.

Pope Leo XIII

~ Pope Leo XIII, *Adiutricem,* Encyclical (September 5, 1895), 4.

~ Pope Leo XIII, *Fidentem piumque animum,* Encyclical (September 20, 1896), 5.

~ Pope Leo XIII, as quoted in Rev. Charles G. Fehrenbach, CSsR, *Mary Day by Day* (New York: Catholic Book Publishing Co., 1987), 144.

~ Pope Leo XIII, *Adiutricem,* 24.

~ Pope Leo XIII, as quoted in Msgr. Joseph A. Cirrincione and Thomas A. Nelson, *The Rosary and the Crisis of Faith* (Charlotte, NC: TAN Books, 1986), 34-35.

~ Pope Leo XIII, *Adiutricem,* 25.

~ Ibid., 26.

~ Ibid., 27.

~ Pope Leo XIII, *Fidentem piumque animum,* 2.

~ Pope Leo XIII, *Iucunda Semper Expectatione,* Encyclical (September 8, 1894), 2.

~ Ibid., 7.

~ Pope Leo XIII, *Laetitiae Sanctae,* Encyclical (September 8, 1893), 18.

~ Pope Leo XIII, *Magnae Dei Matris,* Encyclical (September 8, 1892), 7.

~ Ibid., 18.

~ Ibid., 29.

~ Pope Leo XIII, as quoted in Rev. J.A. Rooney, OP, "Rosary Sunday and Month: The Dominican Portiuncula," *The Rosary Magazine* (October, 1892), p. 453.

~ Pope Leo XIII, *Diuturni Temporis,* Encyclical (September 5, 1898), 3.

~ Pope Leo XIII, *Laetitiae Sanctae,* 16.

~ Pope Leo XIII, *Octobri Mense,* Encyclical (September 22, 1891), 8.

~ Pope Leo XIII, *Diuturni Temporis,* as quoted in *The Rosary of Our Lady: Translations of the Encyclical and Apostolic Letters of Pope Leo XIII,* ed. William Raymond Lawler, OP (Paterson, NJ: St. Anthony Guild Press, 1944), 173-174.

~ Pope Leo XIII, *Letter to the Master General of the Order of Preachers* (September 15, 1883).

~ Bl. James Alberione, *Mary: Hope of the World,* trans. Hilda Calabro, MA (Boston, MA: Daughters of St. Paul, 1981), 156.

~ Bl. James Alberione, *Mary, Mother and Model: Feasts of Mary,* trans. Hilda Calabro, MA (Boston, MA: Daughters of St. Paul, 1958), 203.

~ St. Pope John XXIII, *Grata Recordatio,* Encyclical (September 26, 1959), 2.

Recommended Reading on Pope Leo XIII

~ William Raymond Lawler, OP, ed., *The Rosary of Our Lady: Translations of the Encyclical and Apostolic Letters of Pope Leo XIII* (Paterson, NJ: St. Anthony Guild Press, 1944).

~ *A Light in the Heavens: The Great Encyclical Letters of Pope Leo XIII* (Charlotte, NC: TAN Books, 1995).

~ All 11 Rosary encyclicals of Pope Leo XIII (www.vatican.va).

~ Charles R. Auth, OP, *Rosary Bibliography: English Language Works* (Washington, DC: Dominican House of Studies, 1960).

~ *The Rosary: Papal Teachings.* Texts from 1758-1978, selected and arranged by the Monks of Solesmes (Boston: St. Paul Editions, 1980).

~ Paul A. Böer, Sr., *Enchiridion Sanctissimi Rosarii: A Manual of the Most Holy Rosary* (Veritatis Splendor Publications, 2013).

Blessed Bartolo Longo

* Image on pg. 66: Reprinted with permission of Catholic Online www.catholic.org

~ Bl. Bartolo Longo, as quoted in Ann M. Brown, *Apostle of the Rosary: Blessed Bartolo Longo* (New Hope, KY: New Hope Publications, 2004), 43.

~ Ibid., 53.

~ Bl. Bartolo Longo, as quoted in St. John Paul II, *Rosarium Virginis Mariae*, 15.

~ Bl. Bartolo Longo, as quoted in Ann M. Brown, *Apostle of the Rosary: Blessed Bartolo Longo*, 53.

~ Bl. Bartolo Longo, as quoted in Rory Michael Fox, *Saints, Popes and Blesseds Speak on the Rosary* [E-reader version], 2012.

~ Bl. Bartolo Longo, as quoted in Ann M. Brown, *Apostle of the Rosary: Blessed Bartolo Longo*, 21.

~ Ibid., 51.

~ Bl. Bartolo Longo, as quoted in St. John Paul II, *Beatification Homily of Bl. Bartolo Longo* (October 26, 1980). Trans. Miss Ileana E. Salazar, MA.

~ Bl. Bartolo Longo, *Supplication to the Queen of the Holy Rosary*, as quoted in St. John Paul II, *Rosarium Virginis Mariae*, 43.

~ Bl. Bartolo Longo, as quoted in Barbara Calamari and Sandra DiPasqua, *Visions of Mary* (New York, NY: Harry N. Abrams, Inc., 2004), 82.

~ Bl. Bartolo Longo, as quoted in Ann M. Brown, *Apostle of the Rosary: Blessed Bartolo Longo*, 27.

~ Ibid., 55.

~ Bl. Bartolo Longo, as quoted in Robert Feeney, *The Rosary: "The Little Summa,"* fourth edition (USA: Aquinas Press, 2003), 107.

~ St. John Paul II, *Beatification Homily of Bl. Bartolo Longo.*

~ St. John Paul II, as quoted in Ann M. Brown, *Apostle of the Rosary: Blessed Bartolo Longo,* 47.

~ Pope Benedict XVI, *Homily: Pastoral Visit to the Pontifical Shrine of Pompeii* (October 19, 2008).

~ Ibid.

Recommended Reading on Bl. Bartolo Longo

~ Bl. Bartolo Longo, History of the Sanctuary of Pompeii (Valle di Pompeii: Editing School of Typography of Bartolo Longo, 1895).

~ Bl. Bartolo Longo, *Supplication to the Queen of the Holy Rosary,* as quoted in St. John Paul II, *Rosarium Virginis Mariae,* 43.

~ Bl. Bartolo Longo, *Fifteen Saturdays of the Most Holy Rosary,* trans. Luigi Caturelli (Valle Pompeii, Italy, 1894).

~ Ann M. Brown, *Apostle of the Rosary: Blessed Bartolo Longo* (New Hope, KY: New Hope Publications, 2004).

~ Msgr. Charles M. Mangan, *Blessed Bartolo Longo: Apostle of the Rosary* (Goleta, CA: Queenship Publishing).

Servant of God Joseph Kentenich

~ Servant of God Joseph Kentenich, *Mary, Our Mother and Educator: An Applied Mariology,* trans. Jonathan Niehaus (Waukesha, WI: Schoenstatt Sisters, 1987), 11.

~ Servant of God Joseph Kententich, *The Marian Person,* trans. Jonathan Niehaus. (Waukesha, WI: Schoenstatt Fathers, 2007), 37.

~ Servant of God Joseph Kentenich, *Marian Instrument Piety* (Waukesha, WI: Schoenstatt Center, 1992), 116.

~ Servant of God Joseph Kentenich, *Mary, Our Mother and Educator: An Applied Mariology,* 11.

~ Servant of God Joseph Kentenich, *Talk by Fr. Joseph Kentenich in the Church at Ennabeuren, Germany* (May 3, 1945). Courtesy of Schoenstatt Sisters, Waukesha, WI.

~ Ibid.

~ Ibid.

~ Ibid.

~ Servant of God Joseph Kentenich, *Mary, Our Mother and Educator: An Applied Mariology,* 11.

~ Servant of God Joseph Kentenich, *Heavenwards: Prayers for the Use of the Schoenstatt Family* (Waukesha, WI: Schoenstatt Fathers, 1992), 91.

Recommended Reading on the Servant of
God Joseph Kentenich

~ Servant of God Joseph Kentenich, *Mary, Our Mother and Educator: An Applied Mariology,* trans. Jonathan Niehaus (Waukesha, WI: Schoenstatt Sisters, 1987)

~ Servant of God Joseph Kentenich, *Talk by Fr. Joseph Kentenich in the Church at Ennabeuren, Germany* (May 3, 1945). Original Title: *Unsere Marianische Sendung: Ansprachen in Ennabeuren.* 2 Aufl ed. Horb a. N.: Geiger Druck, 1982.

~ Servant of God Joseph Kentenich, *Exchange of Hearts: The Transforming Power of Consecration to the Immaculate Heart of Mary.* ed., Jonathan Niehaus (Vallendar, Germany: Schoenstatt Fathers, 2012).

~ Fr. Donald H. Calloway, MIC, *The Virgin Mary and Theology of the Body* (Stockbridge, MA: Marian Press, 2005).

~ Fr. Donald H. Calloway, MIC, *Marian Gems: Daily Wisdom on Our Lady* (Stockbridge, MA: Marian Press, 2014).

Servant of God Lúcia Dos Santos

* Image on pg. 79: © Postulação de Francisco e Jacinta Marto.

~ Our Lady to Sr. Lúcia Dos Santos, as quoted in Fr. Robert J. Fox, *2,000 Year Chronology of Mary Through the Ages* (Redfield, SD: Fatima Family Apostolate, 2000), 136.

~ Servant of God Lúcia Dos Santos, *Fatima in Lucia's Own Words* (Fatima, Portugal: Secretariado Dos Pastorinhos, 2011), 50.

~ Servant of God Lúcia Dos Santos, *'Calls' from the Message of Fatima* (Fatima, Portugal: Secretariado dos Pastorinhos, 2000), 134.

~ Servant of God Lúcia Dos Santos, *Fatima in Lucia's Own Words: Volume II.* (Fátima, Portugal: Secretariado dos Pastorinhos, 2006), 106.

~ Servant of God Lúcia Dos Santos, *'Calls' from the Message of Fatima,* 271.

~ Servant of God Lúcia Dos Santos, as quoted in Fr. Robert Fox, *The Intimate Life of Sister Lucia* (USA: Fatima Family Apostolate, 2001), 315.

~ Servant of God Lúcia Dos Santos, as quoted in Rory Michael Fox, *Saints, Popes and Blesseds Speak on the Rosary* [E-reader version], 2012.

~ Servant of God Lúcia Dos Santos, as quoted in Robert Feeney, *The Rosary: "The Little Summa,"* fourth edition (USA: Aquinas Press, 2003), 112.

~ Ibid., 112.

~ Ibid., 114.

~ Servant of God Lúcia Dos Santos, *'Calls' from the Message of Fatima*, 271-272.

~ Servant of God Lúcia Dos Santos, as quoted in Fr. Robert Fox, *The Intimate Life of Sister Lucia*, 316.

~ Ibid., 316.

~ Ibid., 316.

~ Servant of God Lúcia Dos Santos, *A Pathway Under the Gaze of Mary: Biography of Sister Maria Lucia of Jesus and the Immaculate Heart*, trans. James A. Colson (Washington, NJ: World Apostolate of Fatima, 2015), 176.

~ Servant of God Lúcia Dos Santos, as quoted in *The Rosary with Sister Lucia*, trans. James A. Colson (Portugal: Edições Carmelo, 2010), 86.

~ Bl. Gabriele Allegra, *Mary's Immaculate Heart: A Way to God* (Chicago, IL: Franciscan Herald Press, 1985), 54.

Recommended Reading on the Servant of God Lúcia Dos Santos

~ *Fatima in Lucia's Own Words: Sister Lucia's Memoirs. Volume 1.* ed., Fr. Louis Kondor, SVD (Fatima, Portugal: Secretariado Dos Pastorinhos, 2007).

~ *Fatima in Lucia's Own Words: Sister Lucia's Memoirs. Volume 2.* ed., Fr. Louis Kondor, SVD (Fatima, Portugal: Secretariado Dos Pastorinhos, 2006).

~ Servant of God Lucia Dos Santos, *'Calls' from the Message of Fatima* (Fatima, Portugal: Coimbra Carmel, 2000).

~ Carmel of Coimbra, *A Pathway Under the Gaze of Mary: Biography of Sister Maria Lucia of Jesus and the Immaculate Heart*, trans. James A. Colson (Washington, NJ: World Apostolate of Fatima, 2015).

~ Carmel of Coimbra, *The Rosary with Sister Lucia*, trans. James A. Colson (Portugal: Edições Carmelo, 2010).

~ Msgr. Joseph A. Cirrincione and Thomas A. Nelson, *The Rosary and the Crisis of Faith* (Charlotte, NC: TAN Books, 1986).

~ Fr. Robert Fox, *The Intimate Life of Sister Lucia* (USA: Fatima Family Apostolate, 2001).

St. Maximilian Kolbe

* Image on pg. 86: Courtesy of Franciscan Archives, Niepokalanów, Poland. Used with permission.

~ St. Maximilian Kolbe, as quoted in Hilda Elfleda Brown, *She Shall Crush Thy Head: Selected Writings of St. Maximilian Kolbe* (Phoenix, AZ: Leonine Publishers, 2015), 40.

~ Ibid., 40-41.

~ Ibid., 39.

~ Ibid., 119.

~ Ibid., 141.

~ Ibid., 122-123.

~ St. Maximilian Kolbe, *The Writings of St. Maximilian Maria Kolbe*. Vol. II: Various Writings (Lugano, Swizerland: Nerbini International, 2016), no. 1267.

~ St. Maximilian Kolbe, *Scritti di Massimiliano Kolbe* (Roma, 1997), section 1171 [Il Rosario, 1933].

~ St. Maximilian Kolbe, *Scritti di Massimiliano Kolbe* (Roma, 1997), section 505.

~ St. Maximilian Kolbe, *The Writings of St. Maximilian Maria Kolbe*. Vol. II: Various Writings, no. 1088.

~ Ibid., no. 1127.

~ St. Maximilian Kolbe, as quoted in Hilda Elfleda Brown, *She Shall Crush Thy Head: Selected Writings of St. Maximilian Kolbe*, 186.

~ Ibid., 54.

~ Ibid., 42.

~ St. Maximilian Kolbe, *The Writings of St. Maximilian Maria Kolbe*. Vol. II: Various Writings, no.1171.

~ St. Maximilian Kolbe, *Aim Higher*, trans. Fr. Dominic Wisz, OFM Conv. (Libertyville, IL: Marytown Press, 2007), 97.

~ St. Maximilian Kolbe, *Scritti di Massimiliano Kolbe*, section 1171 [Il Rosario, 1933].

~ St. Maximilian Kolbe, *Scritti di Massimiliano Kolbe*, section 1117 [Rycerz Niepokalanej, 1926].

~ St. Maximilian Kolbe, *Scritti di Massimiliano Kolbe*, section 1021 [Grodno 1922-1925; The Archconfraternity of the Holy Rosary].

Recommended Reading on St. Maximilian Kolbe

~ St. Maximilian Kolbe, *The Writings of St. Maximilian Maria Kolbe*. Vol. I: Letters and Vol. II: Various Writings (Lugano, Switzerland: Nerbini International, 2016).

~ St. Maximilian Kolbe, *Aim Higher: Spiritual and Marian Reflections of St. Maximilian Kolbe* (Marytown Press, 1994).

~ Jerzy Domanski, *Maria Was His Middle Name* (Benziger Sisters Publication, 1979).

~ Francis Kalvelage, ed., *Kolbe: Saint of the Immaculata* (San Francisco, CA: Ignatius Press, 2002).

~ Hilda Elfleda Brown, *She Shall Crush Thy Head: Selected Writings of St. Maximilian Kolbe* (Phoenix, AZ: Leonine Publishers, 2015).

Servant of God Frank Duff

~ Servant of God Frank Duff, *Virgo Praedicanda* (Dublin: Mount Salus Press, 1986), 98.

~ Ibid., 101-102.

~ Ibid., 102.

~ Ibid., 101.

~ Ibid., 101.

~ Ibid., 95.

~ Ibid., 97.

~ Ibid., 94.

~ Ibid., 100.

Recommended Reading on the Servant of God Frank Duff

~ *Legio Mariae: The Official Handbook of the Legion of Mary* (Dublin, Ireland: Concilium Legionis Mariae, 1993).

~ Servant of God Frank Duff, *Virgo Praedicanda* (Dublin: Mount Salus Press, 1986).

~ Servant of God Frank Duff, *Walking with Mary: The Spirit of the Legion of Mary* (Glasgow: J.S. Burns, 1956).

~ Servant of God Frank Duff, *The DeMontfort Way* (Montfort Fathers, 1947).

~ Fr. Augustine Hayden, OFM Cap., *Ireland's Loyalty to Mary* (Tralee, Co. Kerry, Ireland: Kerryman Limited, 1952; reprinted in 2016).

Pope Pius XI

* Image on pg. 99: © AS400 DB/Corbis. Used with permission.

~ Pope Pius XI, *Inclytam ac perillustrem* (Letter to R.P. Gillet, Master General of the Dominicans, March 6, 1934)

~ Pope Pius XI, *Inclytam ac perillustrem,* as quoted in Finbar Ryan,

OP (Archbishop of Port of Spain), *Our Lady of Fatima* (Dublin: Richview Press, 1939), 97-99.

~ Pope Pius XI, *Ingravescentibus Malis,* Encyclical (September 29, 1937), 29.

~ Pope Pius XI, as quoted in Rev. Charles G. Fehrenbach, CSsR, *Mary Day by Day* (New York: Catholic Book Publishing Co., 1987), 148.

~ Pope Pius XI, *Ingravescentibus Malis,* 15.

~ Ibid., 9.

~ Pope Pius XI, as quoted in Rev. Charles G. Fehrenbach, CSsR, *Mary Day by Day,* 149.

~ Pope Pius XI, *Ingravescentibus Malis,* 28.

~ Ibid., 12.

~ Ibid., 16.

~ Ibid., 23.

~ Ibid., 22.

~ Pope Pius XI, as quoted in Msgr. Joseph A. Cirrincione and Thomas A. Nelson, *The Rosary and the Crisis of Faith,* 33.

Recommended Reading on Pope Pius XI

~ Pope Pius XI, *Ingravescentibus Malis,* Encyclical (September 29, 1937).

~ Pope Pius XI, *Inclytam ac perillustrem* (Letter to R.P. Gillet, Master General of the Dominicans, March 6, 1934).

~ Pope Pius XI, *Lux Veritatis* (December 25, 1931).

Blessed James Alberione

* Image on pg. 105: Courtesy of Daughters of St. Paul. Used with permission.

~ Bl. James Alberione, *Lord, Teach Us to Pray* (Boston, MA: Daughters of St. Paul, 1982), 222.

~ Ibid., 223.

~ Bl. James Alberione, *Mary, Queen of Apostles* (Boston, MA: Daughters of St. Paul, 1976), 169-170.

~ Ibid., 264.

~ Bl. James Alberione, *Glories and Virtues of Mary,* trans. Hilda Calabro, MA (Boston, MA: Daughters of St. Paul, 1978), 198.

~ Ibid., 200.

~ Bl. James Alberione, *Lord, Teach Us to Pray,* 226-227.

~ Bl. James Alberione, *Glories and Virtues of Mary,* 52.

~ Bl. James Alberione, *Mary, Queen of Apostles,* 180.

~ Ibid., 180.

~ Ibid., 235.

~ Bl. James Alberione, *Glories and Virtues of Mary,* 52.

~ Ibid., 52.

~ Ibid., 46.

~ Ibid., 37.

~ Bl. James Alberione, *Mary, Queen of Apostles,* 179.

~ Bl. James Alberione, *Glories and Virtues of Mary,* 37.

~ Bl. James Alberione, *Mary Leads Us to Jesus: The Marian Spirituality of Blessed James Alberione, SSP.* ed. Marianne Lorraine Trouvé, FSP (Boston, MA: Pauline Books & Media, 2004), 78.

~ Bl. James Alberione, *Mary, Mother and Model: Feasts of Mary,* trans. Hilda Calabro, MA (Boston, MA: Daughters of St. Paul, 1958), 200.

~ Ibid., 200.

~ Ibid., 201.

~ Bl. James Alberione, *Mary, Queen of Apostles,* 32.

~ Ibid., 104.

~ Bl. James Alberione, as quoted in Stephen Lamera, SSP, *James Alberione: A Marvel of Our Times* (Philippines: Daughters of St. Paul, 1977), 157-158.

~ Bl. James Alberione, *Mary: Hope of the World,* trans. Hilda Calabro, MA (Boston, MA: Daughters of St. Paul, 1981), 216.

~ Bl. James Alberione, as quoted in Stephen Lamera, SSP, *James Alberione: A Marvel of Our Times,* 158.

~ Bl. James Alberione, *Glories and Virtues of Mary,* 250.

~ Bl. James Alberione, *Blessed Are the Imitators of Mary Who Bring Jesus to the World,* trans. from his sermons by the Daughters of St. Paul of the USA Province, 24.

~ Ibid., 203.

~ Bl. James Alberione, *Lest We Forget* (Boston, MA: Daughters of St. Paul, 1967), 96.

~ Bl. James Alberione, *Lord, Teach Us to Pray,* 225.

~ Ibid., 226.

~ Ibid., 228.

~ Ibid., 228.

~ Bl. James Alberione (Primo Maestro), *Practices of Piety* (Boston, MA: Daughters of St. Paul), 190.

Recommended Reading on Bl. James Alberione

~ Bl. James Alberione, *Mary, Mother and Model: Feasts of Mary*, trans. Hilda Calabro, MA (Boston, MA: Daughters of St. Paul, 1958).
~ Bl. James Alberione, *Mary, Queen of Apostles* (Boston, MA: Daughters of St. Paul, 1976).
~ Bl. James Alberione, *Glories and Virtues of Mary*, trans. Hilda Calabro, MA (Boston, MA: Daughters of St. Paul, 1978).
~ Bl. James Alberione, *Mary: Hope of the World*, trans. Hilda Calabro, MA (Boston, MA: Daughters of St. Paul, 1981).
~ Bl. James Alberione, *Lord, Teach Us to Pray* (Boston, MA: Daughters of St. Paul, 1982).

Venerable Pope Pius XII

~ Ven. Pope Pius XII, as quoted in Deacon Andrew J. Gerakas, *The Rosary and Devotion to Mary* (Boston, MA: St. Paul Books & Media, 1992), 76.
~ Ven. Pope Pius XII, *Letter to the Most Rev. Master General, Michael Browne, OP, concerning the Marian rosary* (July 11, 1957).
~ Ven. Pope Pius XII, as quoted in Msgr. Joseph A. Cirrincione and Thomas A. Nelson, *The Rosary and the Crisis of Faith* (Charlotte, NC: TAN Books, 1986), 33.
~ Ibid., 33.
~ Ven. Pope Pius XII, *Ingruentium Malorum*, Encyclical (September 15, 1951), 15.
~ Ven. Pope Pius XII, as quoted in Bl. Gabriele Allegra, *Mary's Immaculate Heart: A Way to God* (Chicago, IL: Franciscan Herald Press, 1983), 105.
~ Ven. Pope Pius XII, *Mediator Dei*, Encyclical (November 20, 1947), 173-174.
~ Ven. Pope Pius XII, *Ingruentium Malorum*, 13.
~ Ibid., 14.
~ Ibid., 8.
~ Ven. Pope Pius XII, *Radio address delivered on the 25th anniversary of the apparitions of Our Lady of Fatima* (October 31, 1942).
~ Ven. Pope Pius XII, *Ad Caeli Reginam*, Encyclical (October 11, 1954).
~ Ven. Pope Pius XII, *Radio message to the Marian Congress of the Philippines* (December 5, 1954).

Recommended Readings on Ven. Pope Pius XII

~ Ven. Pope Pius XII, *Bis Saeculari,* Apostolic Constitution (September 27, 1948).

~ Ven. Pope Pius XII, *Ad Caeli Reginam,* Encyclical (October 11, 1954).

~ Ven. Pope Pius XII, *Ingruentium Malorum,* Encyclical (September 15, 1951).

~ Ven. Pope Pius XII, *Letter to Cardinal Griffin, Archbishop of Westminster* (July 14, 1952).

~ Ven. Pope Pius XII, *Fulgens Corona,* Encyclical (September 8, 1953).

~ Sr. M. Pascalina Lehnert, *His Humble Servant: Sister M. Pascalina Lehnert's Memoirs of Her Years of Service to Eugenio Pacelli, Pope Pius XII,* trans. Susan Johnson (South Bend, IN: St. Augustine's Press, 2014).

Servant of God Dolindo Ruotolo

* Image on pg. 122: © Casa Mariana Editrice-Apostolato Stampa. Used with permission.

~ Servant of God Dolindo Ruotolo, *Meditations on the Holy Rosary of Mary,* trans. Giovanna Invitti Ellis (Napoli, Italy, 2006), 36.

~ Ibid., 4.

~ Ibid., 35.

~ Ibid., 5.

~ Ibid., 36.

~ Ibid., 5.

~ Ibid., 41.

~ Ibid., 41.

~ Ibid., 3.

~ Ibid., 4

~ Ibid., 18-19.

~ Ibid., 35.

~ Ibid., 20.

Recommended Reading on the Servant of God Dolindo Ruotolo

~ Servant of God Dolindo Ruotolo, *Meditations on the Holy Rosary of Mary,* trans. Giovanna Invitti Ellis (Napoli, Italy, 2006).

~ Servant of God Dolindo Ruotolo, *A Month with Mary: Daily Meditations for a Profound Reform of Heart in the School of Mary,* trans. Msgr. Arthur B. Calkins (New Bedford, MA: Academy of the Immaculate, 2006).

~ Fr. Donald H. Calloway, MIC, *Rosary Gems: Daily Wisdom on the Holy Rosary* (Stockbridge, MA: Marian Press, 2015).

St. Pio of Pietrelcina

* Image on pg. 127: © Fondazione Voce di Padre Pio – Archivio Fotografico. Used with permission

~ St. Pio of Pietrelcina, as quoted in *Padre Pio: The Wonder Worker,* ed. Francis Mary Kalvelage, FI (New Bedford, MA: Franciscan Friars of the Immaculate, 2009), 67.

~ St. Pio of Pietrelcina, as quoted in Pietro Tartaglia, *The Mysteries of the Rosary and Padre Pio,* second edition (Our Lady of Grace Capuchin Friary: San Giovanni Rotondo, Italy, 1999), 106.

~ Ibid., 10.

~ St. Pio of Pietrelcina, as quoted in *Padre Pio: The Wonder Worker,* 68.

~ St. Pio of Pietrelcina, as quoted in Liz Kelly, *The Rosary: A Path to Prayer* (Chicago, IL: Loyola Press, 2004), 86.

~ St. Pio of Pietrelcina, as quoted in *Padre Pio: The Wonder Worker,* 68.

~ St. Pio of Pietrelcina, as quoted by Most Rev. Paola Carta (Bishop Emeritus of Foggia) in *From the Voice of Padre Pio* (July, 1997). Friary of Our Lady of Grace, San Giovanni Rotondo, Italy.

~ St. Pio of Pietrelcina, as quoted in Gabriel Harty, OP, *The Rosary: The History of my Heart* (Dundalk, Ireland: Dundalgan Press, 2015), 29.

~ St. John Paul II, *Rosarium Virginis Mariae,* 8.

Recommended Reading on St. Pio of Pietrelcina

~ St. Pio of Pietrelcina, as quoted by St. John Paul II in Fr. Robert J. Fox, *First Saturdays for the Triumph of the Immaculate Heart* (Minnesota: Fatima Family Apostolate, 2000).

~ St. Pio of Pietrelcina, *Padre Pio's Words of Hope,* ed. Eileen Dunn Bertanzetti (Huntington, IN: Our Sunday Visitor, Inc., 1999).

~ *Padre Pio: The Wonder Worker,* ed. Francis Mary Kalvelage, FI (New Bedford, MA: Franciscan Friars of the Immaculate, 2009).

St. Josemaría Escrivá

* Image on pg. 132: Courtesy of the Communications Office of Opus Dei. Used with permission.

~ St. Josemaría Escrivá, *Furrow* (New York: Scepter Press, 1986), 265.

~ St. Josemaría Escrivá, *Holy Rosary* (New York, NY: Scepter Press, 2003), 9.

~ St. Josemaría Escrivá, *The Way*, no. 558, p.117, as quoted in Jason Evert, *Purity 365: Daily Reflections on True Love* (Cincinnati, OH: Servant Books, 2009), 105.

~ St. Josemaría Escrivá, *Holy Rosary*, 11.

~ St. Josemaría Escrivá, *Furrow*, 186.

~ Ibid., 186-187.

~ St. Josemaría Escrivá, *Christ is Passing By* (Manila: Sinag-Tala, 1973), 325.

~ St. Josemaría Escrivá, *Friends of God* (New York: Scepter, 1981), 450.

~ St. Josemaría Escrivá, *Holy Rosary*, 12.

~ St. Josemaría Escrivá, *Furrow*, 186.

~ St. Josemaría Escrivá, *Holy Rosary*, 14.

~ St. Josemaría Escrivá, *Friends of God*, 461.

~ St. Josemaría Escrivá, *Holy Rosary*, 15.

Recommended Reading on St. Josemaría Escrivá

~ St. Josemaría Escrivá, *Holy Rosary* (Chicago, IL: Scepter, 1953).

~ St. Josemaría Escrivá, *Christ is Passing By* (Manila: Sinag-Tala, 1973).

~ St. Josemaría Escrivá, *Friends of God* (New York: Scepter Press, 1981).

~ St. Josemaría Escrivá, *The Way: Furrow: The Forge* (New York: Scepter, 2001).

St. Pope John XXIII

* Image on pg. 137: © Universal Images Group North America LLC / DeAgostini / Alamy Stock Photo. Used with permission.

~ St. Pope John XXIII, Letter to Clement Cardinal Micara (September 28, 1960), as quoted in Francis Beauchesne Thornton, *This is the Rosary* (New York: Hawthorn Books, 1961), 10.

~ St. Pope John XXIII, as quoted in Servant of God Patrick Peyton, *All For Her* (Hollywood, CA: Family Theater Productions, 1973), 189.

~ St. Pope John XXIII, as quoted in Jeanne Gosselin Arnold, *A Man of Faith: Father Patrick Peyton, CSC* (Hollywood, CA: Family Theater, Inc., 1983), 133.

~ St. Pope John XXIII, as quoted in Rev. Charles G. Fehrenbach,

CSsR, *Mary Day by Day* (New York: Catholic Book Publishing Co., 1987), 148.

~ St. Pope John XXIII, *Grata Recordatio,* Encyclial (September 26, 1959), 2.

~ St. Pope John XXIII, as quoted in Andrew J. Gerakas, *The Rosary and Devotion to Mary* (Boston, MA: St. Paul Books & Media, 1992), 23.

~ St. Pope John XXIII, *"Radio Message for the Coronation of Our Lady of the Rosary of La Coruña, Spain,"* (September 11, 1960). Trans. Ileana E. Salazar, MA.

~ St. Pope John XXIII, as quoted in Msgr. Joseph A. Cirrincione and Thomas A. Nelson, *The Rosary and the Crisis of Faith* (Charlotte, NC: TAN Books, 1986), 32.

~ St. Pope John XXIII, Letter to Clement Cardinal Micara (September 28, 1960), as quoted in Francis Beauchesne Thornton, *This is the Rosary,* 10.

~ Servant of God Patrick Peyton, as quoted in Laetitia Rhatigan, STD, "The Marian Spirituality of the Servant of God Father Patrick Peyton, C.S.C (1902-1992)," in *Marian Studies,* vol. LXIII (2012), 41.

Recommended Reading on St. Pope John XXIII

~ St. Pope John XXIII, *Grata Recordatio,* Encyclical (September 26, 1959).

~ St. Pope John XXIII, *"Radio Message for the Coronation of Our Lady of the Rosary of La Coruña, Spain,"* (September 11, 1960).

~ St. Pope John XXIII, *Letter to Clemente Cardinal Micara* (September 28, 1960), as quoted in Francis Beauchesne Thornton, *This is the Rosary* (New York: Hawthorn Books, 1961), 9-10.

~ St. Pope John XXIII, *Allocution to the First Pilgrimage of the Living Rosary* (May 4, 1963).

Servant of God Patrick Peyton

* Image on pg. 142: Courtesy of Archives, Holy Cross Family Ministries. North Easton, MA. Used with permission.

~ Servant of God Patrick Peyton, in "Mary, the Pope, and the American Apostle of the Family Rosary," by Fr. Willy Raymond, CSC, in *Behold Your Mother: Priests Speak about Mary,* ed. Stephen J. Rossetti (Notre Dame, IN: Ave Maria Press, 2007), 52.

~ Servant of God Patrick Peyton, as quoted in Jeanne Gosselin Arnold, *A Man of Faith: Father Patrick Peyton, CSC* (Hollywood,

CA: Family Theater, Inc., 1983), 250.
~ Ibid., 34.
~ Servant of God Patrick Peyton, in "Mary, the Pope, and the American Apostle of the Family Rosary," by Fr. Willy Raymond, CSC, in *Behold Your Mother: Priests Speak about Mary,* 53.
~ Servant of God Patrick Peyton, as quoted in Jeanne Gosselin Arnold, *A Man of Faith: Father Patrick Peyton, CSC,* 250.
~ Ibid., 48.
~ Ibid., 63.
~ Ibid., 250.
~ Ibid., 250.
~ Ibid., 268.
~ Servant of God Patrick Peyton, *All For Her* (Hollywood, CA: Family Theater Productions, 1973), 1.
~ Servant of God Patrick Peyton, *Family Prayer* (New York: Benziger Bros., Inc., 1964), 13.
~ Servant of God Patrick Peyton, as quoted in Jeanne Gosselin Arnold, *A Man of Faith: Father Patrick Peyton, CSC,* 27.
~ Ibid., 295.
~ Servant of God Patrick Peyton, as quoted in Laetitia Rhatigan, STD, "The Marian Spirituality of the Servant of God Father Patrick Peyton, CSC (1902-1992)," 31.
~ Servant of God Patrick Peyton, as quoted in *Rosary* [Revised edition of the special rosary issue of *The Immaculate* magazine, 1970], 40. Originally published in October 1965 (Vol. 16. No. 5).
~ Servant of God Patrick Peyton, *Marian Year: 1987-1988* (Albany, NY: The Family Rosary Inc., 1987), 75.

Recommended Reading on the Servant of God Patrick Peyton

~ Servant of God Patrick Peyton, *All For Her* (Hollywood, CA: Family Theater Productions, 1967).
~ Servant of God Patrick Peyton, *Family Prayer* (New York: Benziger Brothers, Inc., 1964).
~ Servant of God Patrick Peyton, *The Ear of God* (Garden City, NJ: Doubleday & Company, Inc., 1951).
~ Jeanne Gosselin Arnold, *A Man of Faith: Father Patrick Peyton, CSC* (Hollywood, CA: Family Theater, Inc., 1983).

Blessed Pope Paul VI

~ Bl. Pope Paul VI, *Marialis Cultus,* Apostolic Exhortation (February 2, 1974), 44.

~ Ibid., 47.

~ Ibid., 46.

~ Bl. Pope Paul VI, *Recurrens Mensis October,* Encyclical (October 7, 1969).

~ Bl. Pope Paul VI, *Marialis Cultus,* 48.

~ Bl. Pope Paul VI, *Mense Maio,* Encyclical (April 29, 1965), 14.

~ Bl. Pope Paul VI, *Marialis Cultus,* 54.

~ Bl. Pope Paul VI, *Christi Matri,* Encyclical (September 15, 1966), 9.

~ Bl. Pope Paul VI, as quoted in Rev. Charles G. Fehrenbach, CSsR, *Mary Day by Day* (New York: Catholic Book Publishing Co., 1987), 150.

~ Bl. Pope Paul VI, as quoted in St. John Paul II, *Rosarium Virginis Mariae,* 12.

~ Bl. Pope Paul VI, *Christi Matri,* 10.

~ Bl. Pope Paul VI, *Marialis Cultus,* 52.

~ Bl. Pope Paul VI, as quoted in Jeanne Gosselin Arnold, *A Man of Faith: Father Patrick Peyton, CSC* (Hollywood, CA: Family Theater, Inc., 1983), 202.

~ Bl. Pope Paul VI, as quoted in *Rosary* (Revised edition of the special rosary issue of *The Immaculate* magazine, 1970), 10. Originally published in October 1965 (Vol.16. No.5).

Recommended Reading on Bl. Pope Paul VI

~ Bl. Pope Paul VI, *Marialis Cultus,* Apostolic Exhortation (February 2, 1974).

~ Bl. Pope Paul VI, *Mense Maio,* Encyclical (April 29, 1965).

~ Bl. Pope Paul VI, *Christi Matri,* Encyclical (September 15, 1966).

~ Bl. Pope Paul VI, *Recurrens Mensis October,* Apostolic Exhortation (October 7, 1969).

~ Bl. Pope Paul VI, *Allocution to the Children of the Living Rosary* (May 10, 1964).

~ Bl. Pope Paul VI, *General Audience* (October 7, 1964).

Venerable Fulton J. Sheen

~ Ven. Fulton J. Sheen, *The World's First Love: Mary, Mother of God* (San Francisco, CA: Ignatius Press, 1996), 207-208.

~ Ibid., 209.
~ Ibid., 210.
~ Ibid., 211.
~ Ibid., 211.
~ Ibid., 215.
~ Ibid., 209.
~ Ibid., 213-214.
~ Ibid., 210.
~ Ibid., 214-215.
~ Ibid., 213.
~ Ibid., 213.
~ Ibid., 214.
~ Ibid., 208.
~ Ibid., 211.

Recommended Reading on Ven. Fulton J. Sheen

~ Ven. Fulton J. Sheen, *The World's First Love: Mary, Mother of God* (San Francisco, CA: Ignatius Press, 1996).

~ Ven. Fulton J. Sheen, *Three to Get Married* (Princeton, NJ: Scepter Publishers, 1951).

~ Peter J. Howard, *The Woman: The Mystery of Mary as Mediatrix in the Teaching of Fulton J. Sheen* (Phoenix, AZ: Leonine Publishers, 2014).

~ Fr. Donald H. Calloway, MIC, *Mary of Nazareth: The Life of Our Lady in Pictures* (San Francisco, CA: Ignatius Press, 2014).

St. Teresa of Calcutta

~ "Our *Lady's words to St. Teresa of Calcutta*," as quoted in Fr. Joseph Langford, MC, *Mother Teresa: In the Shadow of Our Lady* (Huntington, IN: OSV Press, 2007), 60.

~ St. Teresa of Calcutta, *Heart of Joy* (Ann Arbor, MI: Servant Books, 1987.), 19.

~ St. Teresa of Calcutta, as quoted in *Rosary Meditations from Mother Teresa of Calcutta,* ed. V. Lucia (USA: Missionaries of the Blessed Sacrament, 1984).

~ St. Teresa of Calcutta, as quoted in Brian Kolodiejchuk, MC, (ed). *Mother Teresa: Come Be My Light: The Private Writings of the Saint of Calcutta.* (New York: Doubleday, 2007), 141.

~ St. Teresa of Calcutta, *From a Letter to Father Lawrence T. Picachy, S.J., February 13, 1963,* as quoted in Fr. Benedict J. Groeschel, CFR,

The Rosary: Chain of Hope (San Francisco, CA: Ignatius Press, 2003), 16.

~ St. Teresa of Calcutta, as quoted in Susan Conroy, *Praying in the Presence of Our Lord with Mother Teresa* (Huntington, IN: OSV, Inc., 2005), 70.

~ St. Teresa of Calcutta, as quoted in Matthew Kelly, *Rediscover Catholicism* (USA: Beacon Publishing, 2010), 272.

~ St. Teresa of Calcutta, as quoted in Susan Conroy, *Mother Teresa's Lessons of Love & Secrets of Sanctity* (Huntington, IN: OSV Press, 2003), 129.

Recommended Reading on St. Teresa of Calcutta

~ Fr. Brian Kolodiejchuk, MC, ed. *Mother Teresa: Come Be My Light: The Private Writings of the Saint of Calcutta* (New York: Doubleday, 2007).

~ Fr. Joseph Langford, MC, *Mother Teresa: In the Shadow of Our Lady* (Huntington, IN: OSV Press, 2007).

~ Fr. Donald H. Calloway, MIC, *Rosary Gems: Daily Wisdom on the Holy Rosary* (Stockbridge, MA: Marian Press, 2015).

St. John Paul II

~ St. John Paul II, *Angelus Message* (October 29, 1978)

~ St. John Paul II, *Address in Rome* (October 8, 1980)

~ St. John Paul II, *Rosarium Virginis Mariae,* Apostolic Letter (October 16, 2002), 1.

~ Ibid., 40.

~ Ibid., 1.

~ St. John Paul II, *Address at Fatima (May 13, 1982),* as quoted in *John Paul II's Book of Mary,* ed. Margaret R. Bunson (Huntington, IN: OSV Publishing, 1996), 129.

~ St. John Paul II, *Rosarium Virginis Mariae,* 3.

~ St. John Paul II, *Address in Rome (October 8, 1980),* as quoted in *John Paul II's Book of Mary,* 131-132.

~ St. John Paul II, *Rosarium Virginis Mariae,* 3.

~ Ibid., 4.

~ Ibid., 33.

~ Ibid., 5.

~ St. John Paul II, *Angelus message* (October 1, 1995)

~ St. John Paul II, *Rosarium Virginis Mariae,* 41.

~ Ibid., 41.

~ Ibid., 25.

~ Ibid., 26.

~ Ibid., 38

~ Ibid., 39.

~ St. John Paul II, *Angelus message* (September 30, 2001)

~ St. John Paul II, *In Response to questions about the Third Secret whilst speaking in Fulda, Germany (1980)*, as quoted in *Magnificat*, vol. 15, no. 8 (October, 2013), 308.

~ St. John Paul II, *Message to the Bishop of Leiria-Fatima* (October 1, 1997)

~ St. John Paul II, *Rosarium Virginis Mariae*, 15.

~ Ibid., 17.

~ St. John Paul II, *Beatification Homily* (January 21, 1995)

~ St. John Paul II, *Message for the 18th World Youth Day* (April 13, 2003)

~ St. John Paul II, *Rosarium Virginis Mariae*, 43.

~ Pope Benedict XVI, *Angelus* (October 1, 2006)

Recommended Reading on St. John Paul II

~ St. John Paul II, *Rosarium Virginis Mariae*, Apostolic Letter (October 16, 2002).

~ St. John Paul II, *Theotokos: Woman, Mother, Disciple (A Catechesis on Mary, Mother of God)* (Boston, MA: Daughters of St. Paul, 2000).

~ St. John Paul II, *Familiaris Consortio*, Apostolic Exhortation (1981).

~ Margaret R. Bunson, ed., *John Paul II's Book of Mary* (Huntington, IN: OSV Publishing, 1996).

~ Fr. Donald H. Calloway, MIC, *Under the Mantle: Marian Thoughts from a 21st Century Priest* (Stockbridge, MA: Marian Press, 2013).

Pope Benedict XVI

* Image on pg. 175: © Stefano Spaziani. Used with permission.

~ Pope Benedict XVI, *Angelus message* (October 7, 2007).

~ Pope Benedict XVI, *Address at Shrine of Our Lady of Fatima* (May 12, 2010).

~ Pope Benedict XVI, *General Audience* (October 8, 2008).

~ Pope Benedict XVI, *General Audience* (May 1, 2006).

~ Pope Benedict XVI, *Papal Address* (May 3, 2008).

~ Pope Benedict XVI, *Angelus* (October 1, 2006).

~ Pope Benedict XVI, *Angelus message* (October 7, 2012).

~ Pope Benedict XVI, *Homily from Apostolic Journey to Lourdes* (September 14, 2008).

~ Pope Benedict XVI, *Canonization Homily* (October 23, 2005).

~ Pope Benedict XVI, *Papal Address* (June 11, 2011).

~ Pope Benedict XVI, *Angelus message* (October 3, 2010).

~ Pope Benedict XVI, *Homily: Pastoral Visit to the Pontifical Shrine of Pompeii.* (October 19, 2008).

~ Pope Benedict XVI, *General Audience* (October 26, 2005).

~ Pope Benedict XVI, *God and the World: A Conversation with Peter Seewald,* trans. Henry Taylor (San Francisco, CA: Ignatius Press, 2002), 318.

~ Pope Benedict XVI, *General Audience* (February 3, 2010).

Recommended Reading on Pope Benedict XVI

~ Pope Benedict XVI, *Mary* (Spiritual Thoughts Series) (Washington, DC: USCCB, 2008).

~ Pope Benedict XVI, *General Audience* (October 8, 2008).

~ Pope Benedict XVI, *Angelus* (Oct. 1, 2006; Oct. 7, 2008; Oct. 3, 2010; Oct. 7, 2012).

~ Pope Benedict XVI, *Meditation from the Pastoral Visit to Shrine of Pompeii* (October 19, 2008).

HOW TO CHAMPION THE ROSARY

How to Become a Champion of the Rosary

[1] Pope Benedict XVI, *Meditation from the Pastoral Visit to Shrine of Pompeii* (October 19, 2008).

[2] St. Louis de Montfort, *The Secret of the Rosary,* trans. Mary Barbour, TOP (Bay Shore, NY: Montfort Publications, 1988), 103.

[3] Bl. James Alberione, *Lord, Teach Us to Pray* (Boston, MA: Daughters of St. Paul, 1982), 231.

[4] St. Louis de Montfort, *The Secret of the Rosary,* 28.

Why Pray the Rosary?

[1] Pope Leo XIII, *Parta Humano Generi,* Apostolic Letter (September 8, 1901), as quoted in *The Rosary of Our Lady: Translations of the Encyclical and Apostolic Letters of Pope Leo XIII,* ed. William Raymond Lawler, OP (Paterson, NJ: St. Anthony Guild Press, 1944), 195-196.

[2] Pope Leo XIII, *Diuturni Temporis,* Encyclical (September 5, 1898), 3.

[3] St. Louis de Montfort, *The Secret of the Rosary,* 80-81.
[4] Pope Leo XIII, *Supremi Apostolatus Officio, 7.*
[5] Pope Leo XIII, *Laetitiae Sanctae,* Encyclical (September 8, 1893), 3.
[6] St. Louis de Montfort, *The Secret of the Rosary,* 56.
[7] Ven. Fulton J. Sheen, *The World's First Love: Mary, Mother of God* (San Francisco: Ignatius Press, 1996), 208.
[8] Bl. James Alberione, *Mary, Mother and Model: Feasts of Mary,* trans. Hilda Calabro, MA (Boston, MA: Daughters of St. Paul, 1958), 201.

How to Pray the Rosary

[1] St. Louis de Montfort, *God Alone: The Collected Writings of St. Louis de Montfort.* (Bay Shore, NY: Montfort Publications, 1995), 104.
[2] St. Louis de Montfort, *The Secret of the Rosary,* trans. Mary Barbour, TOP (Bay Shore, NY: Montfort Publications, 1988), 93.
[3] Gabriel Harty, OP, *Heaven Sent: My Life Through the Rosary* (Dublin, Ireland: Veritas, 2012), 153.
[4] St. Anthony Mary Claret, *El Colegial Ó Seminarista Teórica y Prácticamente Instruido: Tome I.* (Barcelona, Spain: Librería Religiosa, 1861), 278. Trans. Miss Ileana E. Salazar, MA.
[5] St. Thérèse of Lisieux, as quoted in Romanus Cessario, OP, *Perpetual Angelus: As the Saints Pray the Rosary* (Staten Island, NY: Alba House, 1995), 136.
[6] St. Louis de Montfort, *The Secret of the Rosary,* 91.
[7] Servant of God Dolindo Ruotolo, *Meditations on the Holy Rosary of Mary,* trans. Giovanna Invitti Ellis (Napoli, Italy, 2006), 37.

The 15 Promises of Our Lady to Those Who Pray the Rosary

[1] Servant of God Patrick Peyton, *The Ear of God* (Garden City, NJ: Doubleday & Company, Inc., 1951), 114-115.

Indulgences of the Rosary

[1] St. Louis de Montfort, *The Secret of the Rosary,* trans. Mary Barbour, TOP (Bay Shore, NY: Montfort Publications, 1988), 86.
[2] *Manual of Indulgences: Norms and Grants.* United States Catholic Conference of Bishops Publishing (December 1, 2006).

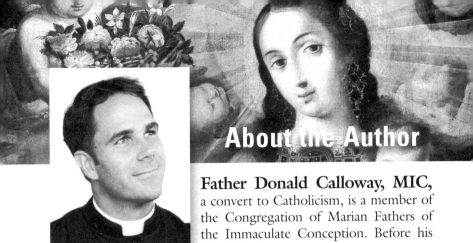

About the Author

Father Donald Calloway, MIC, a convert to Catholicism, is a member of the Congregation of Marian Fathers of the Immaculate Conception. Before his conversion, he was a high school drop-out who had been kicked out of a foreign country, institutionalized twice, and thrown in jail multiple times. After his radical conversion, he earned a BA in philosophy and theology from the Franciscan University of Steubenville, MDiv and STB degrees from the Dominican House of Studies in Washington, D.C., and an STL in Mariology from the International Marian Research Institute in Dayton, Ohio.

In addition to *26 Champions of the Rosary,* he has also written *How to Pray the Rosary* (Marian Press, 2017), the best-selling books *Champions of the Rosary: The History and Heroes of a Spiritual Weapon* (Marian Press, 2016); *Under the Mantle: Marian Thoughts from a 21ˢᵗ Century Priest* (Marian Press, 2013); and *No Turning Back: A Witness to Mercy* (Marian Press, 2010), a bestseller that recounts his dramatic conversion story. He also is the author of the book *Purest of All Lilies: The Virgin Mary in the Spirituality of St. Faustina* (Marian Press, 2008). He introduced and arranged *Marian Gems: Daily Wisdom on Our Lady* (Marian Press, 2014) and *Rosary Gems: Daily Wisdom on the Holy Rosary* (Stockbridge, MA: Marian Press, 2015). Further, he has written many academic articles and is the editor of two books: *The Immaculate Conception in the Life of the Church* (Marian Press, 2004) and *The Virgin Mary and Theology of the Body* (Marian Press, 2005).

Father Calloway is the Vicar Provincial and Vocation Director for the Mother of Mercy Province.

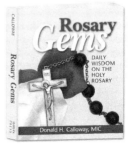

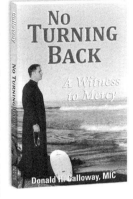

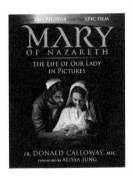

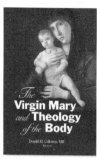

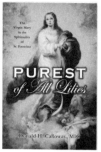

The Virgin Mary and Theology of the Body
Paperback. 285 pages.
Y70-TVM

The Immaculate Conception in the Life of the Church
Paperback. 198 pages.
Y70-ICLC

Purest of All Lilies: The Virgin Mary in the Spirituality of St. Faustina
Paperback. 128 pages.
Y70-POAL

Champions of the Rosary T-Shirt

Show your love of the Rosary with this t-shirt bearing the cover image of Fr. Donald Calloway's *Champions of the Rosary* — the perfect gift for those who want to spread their love for this devotion! T-shirts are black cotton/ polyester blend and come in a variety of sizes.

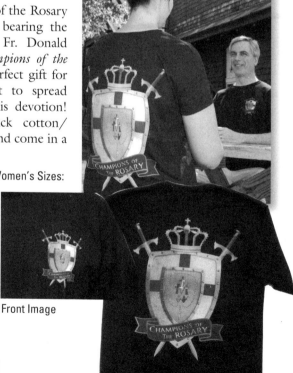

Product Codes for Women's Sizes:
Y70-FCRS (small)
Y70-FCRM (med)
Y70-FCRL (large)
Y70-FCRXL (x-large)
Y70-FCRXXL (xx-large)

Product Codes for Men's Sizes:
Y70-MCRS (small)
Y70-MCRM (med)
Y70-MCRL (large)
Y70-MCRXL (x-large)
Y70-MCRXXL (xx-large)

Front Image

Back Image

Call 1-800-462-7426 or visit www.fathercalloway.com

Champions of the Rosary
in Canvas Art

Commissioned by Fr. Donald Calloway, "The 26 Champions of the Rosary" image was painted by artist Maria Madonna Bouza Urbina in 2016. Now available on canvas, the image depicts the Blessed Mother holding the rosary and a sword, surrounded by 26 individuals who made the rosary central to their very being. Father Calloway tells the stories of how they lived out their love for this devotion in his book. Image size is 10" x 18".

Canvas image with Champions of the Rosary: Y70-RC10GW

Canvas image with names of 26 Champions of the Rosary: Y70-CR10GW

Canvas image with Queen of the Rosary in Black and White: Y70-BW10GW

Canvas image with Queen of the Rosary in Color: Y70-QR10GW

Call 1-800-462-7426 or visit www.fathercalloway.com

Thirteenth of the Month Club

Father Donald Calloway, MIC, Marian vocation director, participates in a recurring feature in the Thirteenth of the Month Club newsletter.

I'm honored and delighted to do this for the club, since it's a good way for me to help people come to a better place in their relationship with Our Lady. I want to let people know that by being in the Thirteenth of the Month Club, they're part of the Marian family. They are praying for us [the Marian Fathers of the Immaculate Conception], and we are praying for them.

Thirteenth of the Month Club members are a group of special friends who help support the work of the Marian Fathers of the Immaculate Conception. On the 13th of each month, members pray the Rosary for the intentions of the Club. The Marians residing in Fatima offer a special Mass on the 13th of the month for members' intentions.

All members pledge a monthly gift and receive the Club newsletter, published by the Association of Marian Helpers, Stockbridge, MA 01263.

Call: 1-413-298-1382 or
visit marian.org/13th
E-mail: thirteenth@marian.org

MARY 101 Kit
Know Our Lady. Love Our Lady.

Y70-MKIT

This is your one-stop introduction to the Blessed Virgin Mary. Get to know our spiritual mother better with information on the basic Church dogmas about Mary Immaculate, key prayers such as the Rosary, and answers to common Protestant objections to devotion to Mary.

In our special 100th Anniversary of Fatima pack (included in the kit), we provide resources to help you learn about the apparitions and calls of Our Lady at Fatima, why these apparitions are still relevant today, and what we can do to bring about peace in the world.

Call 1-800-462-7426 or visit ShopMercy.org

Marian Press pamphlets on Mary

Devotion to Mary

A. The Hail Mary Y70-HML

B. Practice of the Three Hail Marys and Efficacious Novena
Y70-POTE

C. I Am the Lady of the Rosary
Y70-ILR

D. Novena to Our Lady of Guadalupe Y70-NOLG

E. A Dream Come True
Written by Fr. Donald H. Calloway, MIC. Y70-MOGP

F. Graces Offered by the Brown Scapular Y70-GOBS

G. The Blue Scapular Y70-BLS

Pray the Rosary Daily Pamphlet

"Pray the Rosary Daily" is a beautifully illustrated guide to praying the Rosary. Over a million sold every year! "Pray the Rosary Daily" also includes St. John Paul II's reflections on all four sets of mysteries of the Rosary. Y70-PR2

Marians of the Immaculate Conception Rosary Gift Sets

This rosary was designed exclusively for the Marian Fathers of the Immaculate Conception. It reflects our mission to spread devotion to Mary Immaculate. Each set comes enclosed in a matching gift box. Y70-OMR3

Call 1-800-462-7426 or visit ShopMercy.org

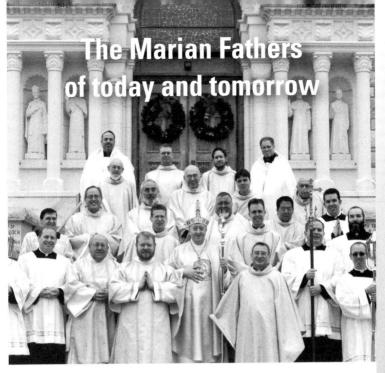

The Marian Fathers of today and tomorrow

Marian Fathers of the Immaculate Conception

What are you looking for in the priests of tomorrow?

- ☑ Zeal for proclaiming the Gospel
- ☑ Faithfulness to the Pope and Church teaching
- ☑ Love of Mary Immaculate
- ☑ Love of the Holy Eucharist
- ☑ Concern for the souls in Purgatory
- ☑ Dedication to bringing God's mercy to all souls

These are the top reasons why men pursuing a priestly vocation are attracted to the Congregation of Marian Fathers of the Immaculate Conception.

Please support the education of these future priests. Nearly 150 Marian seminarians are counting on your gift.

1-413-298-1382
marian.org/helpseminarians

Give a Consoling Gift: *Prayer*

Marian Helpers